The Pepper Lady's Pocket Pepper Primer

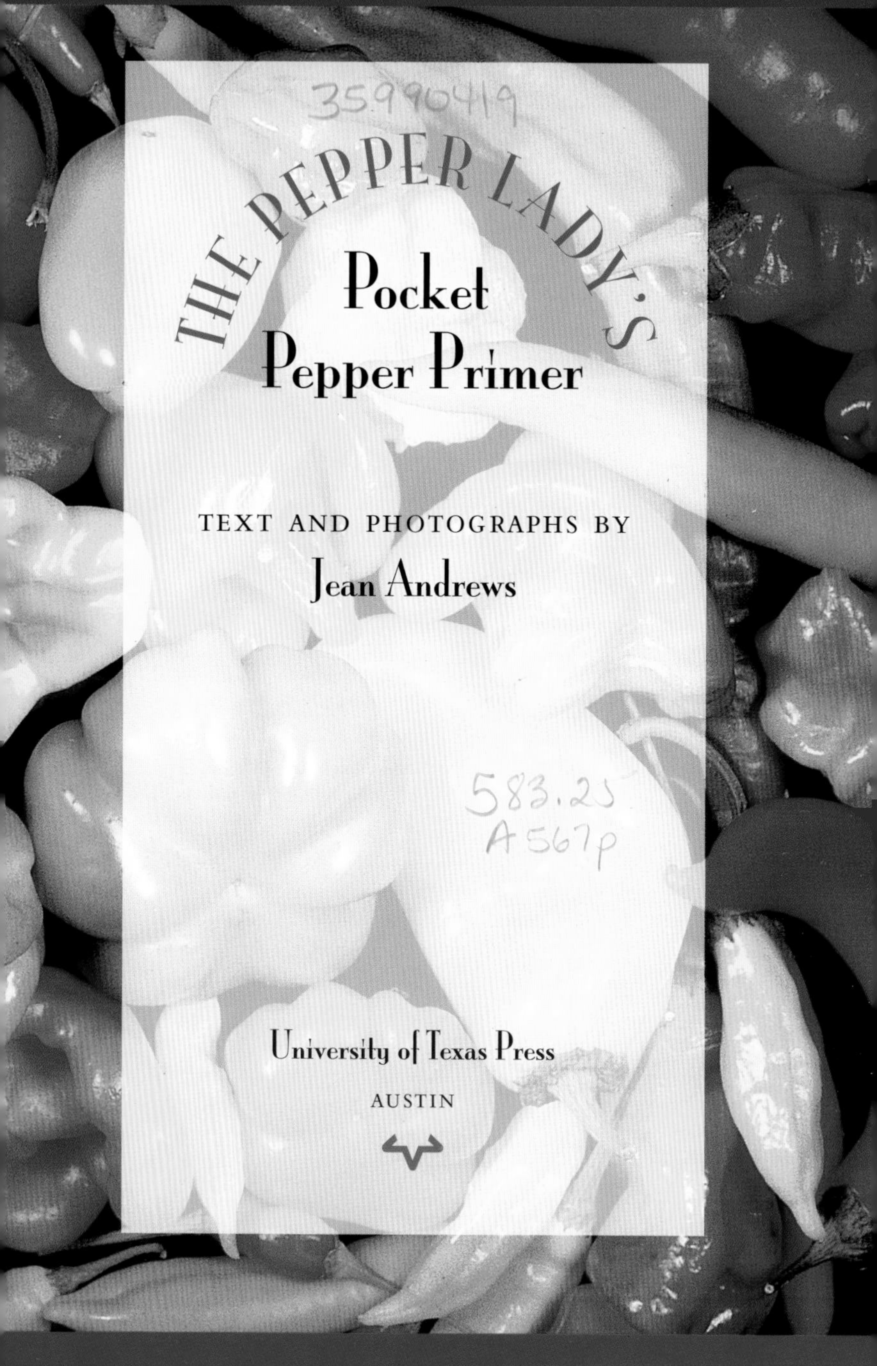

THE PEPPER LADY'S Pocket Pepper Primer

TEXT AND PHOTOGRAPHS BY

Jean Andrews

University of Texas Press

AUSTIN

The Pepper Lady® is a registered trademark belonging to Jean Andrews.

Printed in China

First edition, 1998

♾ The paper used in this publication meets the minimum requirements of American National Standard for Information Sciences—Permanence of Paper for Printed Library Materials, ANSI Z39.48-1984.

Designed by Ellen McKie

LIBRARY OF CONGRESS
CATALOGING-IN-PUBLICATION DATA

Andrews, Jean
The Pepper Lady's pocket pepper primer / text and photographs by Jean Andrews. — 1st ed.
p. cm.
Includes index.
ISBN 0-292-70483-6 (pbk.)
1. Peppers—Identification. I. Title.
QK495.S7A53 1997
583'.25—dc21 96-51216

Dedicated to
Peter Piper

CONTENTS

The Pepper Lady's Pocket Pepper Primer

With their infinite variety, peppers are the seashells of the plant kingdom.

WHO PICKED THOSE PICKLED PEPPERS?

Introduction

OK, so Peter Piper picked a peck of pickled peppers, but he could not have done it if it had not been for the dauntless Christopher Columbus. Columbus may not have been the first denizen of the Old World to set foot in the New World, but his initial hazardous voyage not only set in motion the reuniting of the two worlds that had drifted apart eons earlier but also initiated the Age of Discovery. If that was not enough to assure his place in history, all the Columbus detractors in the world cannot take from him the undisputed credit for being the first European to introduce red peppers, the fiery spice native to that strange New World environment, to the inhabitants of the Iberian peninsula. He carried samples of those blistering fruits which were used by the pre-Columbian people of Mesoamerica and South America to flavor their foods to show to his royal supporters in Spain on his return from his first voyage of exploration. Offering them examples of the many new flora, he reported that "All the trees were as different from ours as day from night and so the fruits, the herbage, the rocks, and all things." Certainly the blistering red pods were convincing evidence of that radical difference.

Although he never admitted it, Columbus did not find the East Indies or the Far Eastern spices. He had sailed west in search of a direct route to Asia so that the sovereigns of

Spain, Ferdinand and Isabella, could establish unobstructed sea routes to trading ports in the spice-growing regions and thereby evade the Moslem monopoly of that trade with the Far East. The Catholic rulers coveted a major share of the vast revenue produced by the spice trade so that they could finance their continuous battles against the Moors. So confident in his findings was Columbus that he called the lands he encountered during his four voyages from 1492 to 1502 the Indies, and the people who inhabited those lands he designated as Indians. The pungent spice (*Capsicum*) which he found them eating on everything they consumed he called *pimiento* (pepper) after *pimienta,* the pungent black pepper (*Piper nigrum*) from India, which he was looking for. Confusion over what to call the new pepper has prevailed since he wrote of it in his first journal on January 1, 1493, from a spot he named Navidad on the island of Española (Haiti and Dominican Republic). This little book is intended to clarify some of the lingering confusion surrounding the pungent pods indigenous to Columbus' New World.

How to Use This Book

This book is designed for pepper lovers of all types, professional or not—chefs, food writers, gardeners, vendors, and what-have-you—to be used in the kitchen, food market, office, plant nursery, seed house, or any place one might be trying to identify a pepper. This is not a recipe book or a book giving extensive background information—I have done that in the books *Peppers: The Domesticated Capsicums* (Austin: University of Texas Press, New Edition, 1995) and *Red Hot Peppers* (New York: Macmillan Publishing Co., 1993). The first is considered to be the most complete work on the genus *Capsicum,* and the second is equally exhaustive on the food aspect of that genus, and includes two hundred recipes. There are other books, too numerous to mention, with excellent recipes using peppers. Here, in this book, we're dealing with *identification.*

Correct identification is important because each pepper variety or group/type (see pages 15–19) has specific qualities unique to that variety or group/type, such as flavor, color, aroma, pungency, size, thickness of flesh, etc. If a pepper group/type with different characteristics is substituted in a recipe, the results will not be those intended by the recipe creator. You cannot switch pepper types/groups promiscuously and expect the dish you are preparing to come out right; however, the cultivars within a type/group are interchangeable for the most part. Unfortunately, the prospective pepper user cannot depend on the labels placed on peppers in food markets or even on what the grower at the farmer's market might say. It is important for the purchaser to recognize the pepper correctly regardless of what written labels and/or vendors claim, not only to be able to recognize it visually and know its most prevalent common name, but also to be able to distinguish the differences in taste, smell, and feel.

Each of the forty-five peppers in this book is discussed individually and is listed in alphabetical order according to common type/group name. If the dried state of a pepper is consistently known by a different name from the fresh one, it is listed under that name. The scientific name is given under the common name. Where each pepper is described, a photograph shows it in size relative to the other peppers in the book.

For quick reference, the information concerning each pepper is arranged in a consistent form using uniform categories. Size, the most critical visual reference, is first, followed by color, fruit shape, flesh, pungency, substitutes, other names, sources, uses, and remarks. Entire fruit shape at peduncle (stem) attachment, fruit shape at blossom end or apex, and fruit cross-section corrugation are shown in the illustrated glossary on page 161. An explanation of fruit group/types is presented on page 15. A Pungency Rating Heat Scale can be found on page 31. In the "Substitutes" and "Uses" categories, cooks can find what other peppers may be substituted along with suggestions of how to use the variety being described. Under "Sources," you can learn where to locate both dried and fresh peppers, prepared products, and the seed. In addition, the list of Seed Sources on pages 171–172 contains a few addresses to help you with your search, although peppers have become so widespread and their use so popular that most large food stores are well supplied. You should have no problem finding the pepper you are looking for or one of its substitutes suggested herein. At the end of each description I have made some personal remarks based on my observations during years of studying peppers, growing them, cooking with them, and traveling worldwide in quest of the captivating *Capsicum*.

MANY THANKS TO:

José Marmolejo, owner of Don Alfonso (imported dried peppers), dauntless growers Richard and Robert Penn at Sunset Farms, and professor/gardeners Joe Colwell and Richard Willis, all of Austin, Texas, as well as Professor W. Hardy Eshbaugh, Miami University, Oxford, Ohio, and Petoseed Company, especially Jim Lusk, of Saticoy, California, who loaned their photos when all else failed me. They made this guide possible by helping me with collecting and growing the peppers I photographed for this handbook. I consider each a valued friend and true pepper *aficionado.*

WHAT'S IN A NAME?

Nomenclature

In 1492 the first Europeans heard the Caribbean Arawaks, Columbus' Indians, calling the pungent *Capsicum* fruit *axí*, the South American name they brought with them when they migrated north to the Antilles with the fruit. The Spanish transliterated the Arawak word to *ají* (*ajé, agí*). The Spanish themselves never adopted that Arawak word in either the West Indies or North America, and now both the Arawaks and their language are extinct. Instead the Spanish used *pimiento*, a variation of *pimienta*, their own name for the pungent pepper of India they were seeking.

Today in the Dominican Republic (formerly Española) and a few other places in the Caribbean, along with much of South America, the pungent varieties are still called *ají*. However, *uchu* and *huayca* are other ancient words used for capsicums by some Amerindian groups in the Andean area. In Spain, American peppers are called *pimiento* or *pimentón* (depending on the size), after *pimienta* or black pepper from India. However, the Spanish names did not stay with the plant through Europe; for example, it is called *peperone* in Italy, *piment* in France, and *paprika* by the Slavic peoples in the Balkans.

It was not until 1518, a quarter of a century later when the Spanish arrived in Mexico, that they heard Nahuatl-speaking natives call the fiery red fruit, which their ancestors had domesticated, *chilli.* The Nahuatl stem *chil* refers to the chilli plant. It also means "red." To the generic word *chilli*, the term that described the particular chilli cultivar was added (e.g., *Tonalchilli* = chilli of the sun or summer, *Chiltecpin* = flea chilli). In Mexico today, the Spanish word *chile*, which was derived from *chilli*, refers to both pungent and sweet types and is used in the Nahuatl style combined with a descriptive adjective, such as *chile colorado* (red chilli) or with a word that indicates the place of origin, such as *chile poblano* (chilli from Puebla). The same Mexican variety can have different names in different geographic regions, in various stages of maturity, or in the dried state, which makes for additional confusion. Common names are not reliable because they are so variable.

The Portuguese language uses *pimenta* for peppers and qualifies the various types—*pimenta-da-caiena*, cayenne pepper; *pimenta-da-malagueta*, red pepper; *pimenta-do-reino*, black pepper; *pimenta-da-jamaica*, allspice—while *pimentão* is pimento, red pepper, or just pepper. *Ají* and *chile* are not found in a Portuguese dictionary, nor did the Portuguese carry those words with them in their travels.

Later the Dutch and the English were probably responsible for carrying the current capsicum names to the East. In Australia, India, Indonesia, and Southeast Asia in general, *chilli* (*chillies*) or sometimes *chilly* is used by English speakers for the pungent types, while the mild ones are called capsicums. Each Far Eastern language has its own word for chillies—*prik* in Thai, *mirch* in Hindi, to name but two. Most have no name for sweet peppers.

The most confusion exists in the United States. Here we find both *chili* (*chilies*), one of the anglicized spellings, and the Spanish *chile* (*chiles*) used by some for the pungent fruits of the *Capsicum* plant, while *chili* is also used as a short form of *chili con carne*, a variously concocted mixture of meat and chillies. American academicians writing in scholarly journals use *chili pepper*, which is unconfused but redundant and lengthy. The *Oxford English Dictionary* gives *chilli* as the primary usage, calling *chile* and *chili* variants. *Webster's New International Dictionary* prefers *chili* followed by the Spanish *chile* and the Nahuatl *chilli*. Most English-speaking people outside the United States use *chilli*.

The spelling *chilli* was first used in print by Dr. Francisco Hernández (1514–1578), the first European to collect plants systematically in the New World. In his writings in Spanish published early in the seventeenth century, he interpreted the Nahuatl name for capsicums as *chilli*. That Spanish spelling was later changed to *chile* by Spanish-speaking Mexicans. The Food and Agriculture Organization of the United Nations (FAO) has as one of its goals consistency in nomenclature. In its publications pungent capsicums are called *chillies* and sweet capsicums are *peppers*.

Not because one name is right and another is wrong, but for the sake of consistency and clarity it would help if *capsicums* or *peppers* were used when speaking of the fruit of the *Capsicum* in general, both sweet and pungent; *chilli* for the pungent types; *chili* for the spicy meat dish; and *pimento* for the sweet, thick-fleshed, heart-shaped red capsicum. *Chile* in italics should refer to a native Mexican cultivar or, not italicized, to the long green/red or Anaheim/New Mexican Chile type. **Whenever possible, the name of the specific fruit type/group or variety/cultivar should be used.**

In my humble, Quixotic opinion, the original *chilli* is not only the logical English spelling but also the correct one, especially when writing for a global audience. *Chili* would be second. Perhaps the taxonomist's rule of precedence for scientific names should be applied to this vernacular problem in order to settle the issue. Think about it! To my dismay, the growing usage and acceptance of the Spanish word *chile* is, nevertheless, further proof that so-called standard English is constantly changing. There is a growing population which cannot speak either Spanish or English without the help of the other.

Until archaeologists find evidence to the contrary, capsicums can hold the claim to being the first spice to be consumed by humans. Today, seven thousand years later, more than one-fourth of the inhabitants of planet earth eat peppers every day of their lives . . . that's a lot of folk. In fact, chilli is the most cultivated and popular spice and condiment in the world today. Most contemporary Old World *Capsicum* consumers do not realize that their ancestors did not have the opportunity to enjoy that pungent additive before the sixteenth century because it did not grow in their world. They did not have red pepper until after the Portuguese acquired the seeds from some yet undetermined Spanish source and carried those seeds to existing Portuguese colonies, such as Guinea, in tropical West Africa. A royal decree required every Portuguese ship, even those in Brazil, to return to Lisbon to start its voyage to the Far East. Consequently, for more than a century and a half after the Discovery, it was from those closer Portuguese colonies, and not directly from the New World, that the new "Ginnie" peppers went to East Africa and the western coast of India, and later to Portuguese markets in Antwerp and England. From the Malabar Coast of India the New World capsicums were added to the cargoes of Old World spice traders who sailed the traditional ancient routes to the Far East, plodded in caravans along the fabled Silk Roads, or followed the medieval Middle Eastern routes where peppers were promptly noticed, along with corn, beans, and squash, by the Ottoman Turks. The leaders of the conquering Ottoman armies knew a good thing when they saw it, and soon the easily grown, tasty, and highly nutritious new plants in this critical food complex were being cultivated to feed both men and horses of the vast Turkish legions on their forays into their far-flung empire, which included the Balkans, the Middle East, Egypt, and North Africa. The savvy merchants of Venice serving European markets were quick to get in on the Middle Eastern trade, and it was within fifty years of Columbus' first voyage that the "Columbian Exchange" was an established thing and peppers had spread to almost every inhabited land with the likely exception of

North America above the Rio Grande, Polynesia, Australia, and New Zealand. During that period most Europeans and Orientals were not aware of the American origin of capsicums. By 1600, when other European nations began to wrest control of the spice trade from the Portuguese, the diffusion of *Capsicum* peppers and other New World foods to Africa, the Middle East, Central Asia, the Far East, and Europe was complete. On December 2, 1621, peppers first arrived in Virginia from England via Bermuda, making their circumnavigation of the globe entire.

Cultivar Names

In the *International Code of Nomenclature of Cultivated Plants—1969*, which regulates the naming of agricultural, horticultural, and silvicultural cultivars only and not genera or species, we are told that a variety or cultivar is an assemblage of cultivated plants which is clearly distinguished by any characters and which, when reproduced, retains those distinguishing characters. A variety which originated and persisted under cultivation (grown by humans) is called a cultivar. The cultivar is the lowest category under which names are recognized. The term was derived by combining the terms *cultivated* and *variety*. Here is a brief taxonomic review as it relates to peppers—take it or leave it.

Cultivated plants are named at three main levels: genus, species, and cultivar (variety).

A genus is a subdivision of a family with one or more closely related species. Names at the genus (generic) level are botanical generic names and common names used in a generic sense. All the red and green peppers in the world are in the genus *Capsicum*. Black pepper is in a genus of another family.

A species is a division of a genus consisting of individuals with common ancestry which interbreed in nature. Names at the species (specific) level are botanical and common names of species. The botanical specific name, written in a Latin form, is a binary combination (binomial) consisting of the name of the genus followed by a single specific epithet (see pages 21–25 for the species of *Capsicum*).

A cultivar name, when immediately following a botanical or common name, must be distinguished clearly from the latter, either by placing the abbreviation cv. before the cultivar name, or by some typographic device, such as enclosing it within single quotation marks if it is a registered name. Cultivar names are not Latinized, and double quotation marks or the abbreviation var. should never be used to distinguish them. Each word in a cultivar name should be capitalized except when linguistic usage demands otherwise.[1] For example: *Capsicum chinense* cv. 'Red Savina.'

The breeder who developed a particular cultivar is the owner of the immediate breeding material from which the new cultivar was developed. The legitimate name must be accepted by a registration authority and included in a statutory register. A statutory registration authority is a body

[1]Between 1978 and 1984 while I was preparing the manuscript and paintings for the first edition of my book *Peppers: The Domesticated Capsicums,* I lived in a small South Texas city and had no one to help me with nomenclatural problems. Even my editor was not familiar with the rules controlling the writing of botanical names. As a consequence in the captions under my paintings I used common names (names of group/types) as varietal epithets. Michael Nee of the New York Botanical Garden pointed this out in a most kind manner, and taxonomist Billie L. Turner, the director of the Herbarium at the University of Texas at Austin, helped to resolve the difficulty I was having with botanical nomenclature. Later editions were corrected. I hope this discussion will help any interested readers who don't have the time or sources to dig it out for themselves.

responsible for registration established by legal enactment of a particular country, or by legal treaty between countries. In some countries, names which may be used for cultivars are trademarked.

Each cultivar has one correct name, the name by which it is internationally known. For a name to be legitimate (names after January 1, 1959) it must be validly published or have been accepted by a registration authority. A cultivar name must remain unchanged when and if the botanical name is changed. A cultivar name should be attached to a common name only if the common name is widely known.

Capsicum Cultivars by Group/Type

By definition in a dictionary of biology a variety is a group or type within a species or subspecies which differs in some significant respect from other members of the species. The name given to the group/type is actually the common or generic name for its qualified members. When a species includes many cultivars, assemblages of similar cultivars may be designated as groups or types. I'll use *group/type* to reduce confusion. How many "named" roses or apples can you think of? Each of them is a cultivar of some particular group/type of rose or apple.

The classification of group/types used here is based on that of P. G. Smith, B. Villalon, and P. L. Villa (*Hortscience* 1987, 22[1]: 11–13), which was directed toward a rational horticultural classification of the commercially significant cultivars in the United States. Since it was published in 1987, interest in peppers has greatly increased, with the result that now there is a wider assortment of cultivars being grown. Then, they included only a few Mexican cultivars and only one species other than *Capsicum annuum* var. *annuum*. I have expanded on that classification and tried to place each pepper described in this book in an appropriate group/type. Cultivars of each group/type are listed within its description.

I. FRUIT LARGE, SMOOTH, THICK-FLESHED
Capsicum annuum var. *annuum*

A. Bell group/type
Fruit large, blocky, blunt, 3- to 4-lobed. Mostly nonpungent, although a few pungent forms have been developed.

1. Bell pepper and its many cultivars

B. Pimento group/type
Fruit heart-shaped but pointed or tomato-shaped, smooth, thick-walled, nonpungent.

1. Pimento and its cultivars
2. Tomato pepper and its cultivars

II. FRUIT BROAD, SMOOTH, THIN-WALLED
Capsicum annuum var. *annuum*

A. Poblano/Ancho group/type
Fruit broad-shouldered, pointed, thin-walled, somewhat flattened, stem indented into top of fruit-forming cup, sweet to mildly pungent.

1. Poblano and its cultivars, fresh
2. Ancho and its cultivars, dried
3. Mulato and its cultivars, dried

III. FRUIT LONG, SLENDER
Capsicum annuum var. *annuum*

A. Anaheim, New Mexican Chile, Long Green/Long Red Chile group/type
Moderately pungent to pungent.

1. Anaheim/New Mexican and its cultivars
2. Chilaca, fresh Pasilla
3. Chilcoztli
4. Pasilla and its cultivars, dried

B. Cayenne group/type

Pungent, pointed.

1. Cayenne and its cultivars
2. De Arbol
3. Guajillo, dried
4. Mirasol, fresh
5. Japonés
6. Romesco
7. Thai

C. Ethnic/Cuban group/type

Sweet to moderately pungent.

1. Cuban, ex. 'Cubanelle'
2. Italian, ex. 'Pepperoncini'
3. Eastern European-Balkan, ex. 'Romanian'

IV. FRUIT ELONGATED TO 7.5 CM, LONG, GREEN WHEN IMMATURE; PUNGENT
Capsicum annuum var. *annuum*

A. Jalapeño group/type

1. Jalapeño and its cultivars

B. Serrano group/type

1. Serrano and its cultivars

C. Small, elongate-conical, pungent group/type

Slender, medium to thin-walled, highly pungent, green to red.

1. Catarina
2. Turkish
3. Costeño

D. Small, elongate, green to red or yellow, pungent group/type

Folded or retracted apex, medium to thin-walled, pungent.

1. Peter (Penis) pepper

E. Very small, globular to elongate, pungent group/type

Round to ovoid, thin-walled, highly pungent, green to red or blackish.

1. Chiltepín

F. Elongate, conical, thin-walled, highly pungent, green to red

1. Chilpequín

V. FRUIT SMALL (TO 5 CM), GLOBULAR TO OBLATE, THICK FLESH; SWEET TO PUNGENT
Capsicum annuum var. *annuum*

A. Cherry pepper group/type

1. Sweet Cherry
2. Hot Cherry
3. Cascabel

B. Squash pepper group/type

1. Squash pepper

VI. FRUIT WAXY SMOOTH, USUALLY YELLOW WHEN IMMATURE; SWEET TO PUNGENT
Capsicum annuum var. *annuum*

A. Small wax with yellow stage group/type

1. 'Cascabella'
2. 'Santa Fe Grande'/Caribe
3. 'Caloro'
4. 'Floral Gem'

B. Small wax with yellow-green stage group/type

1. 'Fresno'

C. Long wax group/type

1. Banana pepper, sweet
2. Hungarian Wax, pungent

VII. FRUIT SLENDER, ERECT, THIN-WALLED, SMOOTH; PUNGENT; OF THE SPECIES *Capsicum frutescens*

A. Tabasco group/type

1. 'Greenleaf Tabasco'
2. 'Select Tabasco'
3. 'Tabasco'

VIII. FRUIT LONG, SLENDER, POINTED, THIN-WALLED; PUNGENT; OF THE SPECIES *Capsicum baccatum* var. *pendulum* AND *Capsicum chinense*

A. Andean Ají group/type

Pungent.

1. Cusqueño
2. Puca-uchu
3. Ají Limón
4. Ají Oro
5. Dátil

IX. CAMPANULATE, UNDULATING, THIN-WALLED, POINTED OR ROUNDED APEX, TRUNCATE AT PEDUNCLE ATTACHMENT; MILD TO VERY PUNGENT; OF THE SPECIES *Capsicum baccatum* var. *pendulum* AND *Capsicum chinense*

A. Habanero group/type

Somewhat elongated; very pungent.

1. Habanero
2. West Indian Hot

B. Scotch Bonnet group/type

Low and pungent

1. Ají Flor
2. Rocotillo
3. Scotch Bonnet, rounded apex

KNOW YOUR POISON!

How to Recognize the Domesticated Species

How do you account for the popularity of the pepper pod—neither pepper nor a pod? The genus *Capsicum* is a rather mixed-up group of plants. *Capsicum* consists of perennial herbaceous to woody shrubs native to the American tropics. In areas subject to freezes, it is grown as an annual. It originated somewhere in southwestern Brazil or in central Bolivia. Long before humans migrated across the Bering Strait to America, and before that migration reached Mesoamerica, it had been carried by birds, its natural means of dispersal, to other parts of South America. Centuries later, when the Europeans arrived, not only had birds and/or pre-Columbian Amerindians carried the indigenous spice to Mesoamerica and the Caribbean; they had also domesticated the four or five species which are cultivated today.

All species of the wild (undomesticated) *Capsicum* have certain common characters: small pungent, red fruits which may be round, elongate, or conical; fruit that is attached to the plant in an erect position; fruit that is readily removed from the calyx; and seeds that are dispersed by birds. All mild and sweet capsicums are the result of domestication.

There are four or five domesticated species: *Capsicum annuum* var. *annuum*, *C. frutescens*, *C. chinense*, *C. baccatum* var. *pendulum*, and *C. pubescens*. *Capsicum annuum* var. *annuum*,

ABOVE: *Capsicum annuum* var. *annuum*
BELOW: *C. chinense*

BELOW: *C. baccatum* var. *pendulum*
OPPOSITE: *C. pubescens*

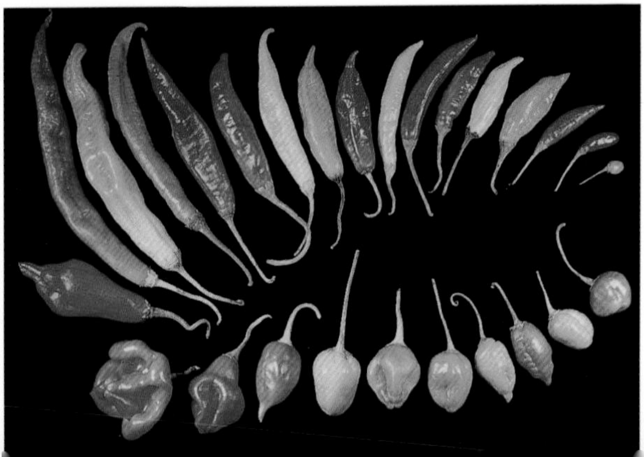

C. frutescens, and *C. chinense* are the only ones that became established in the Old World, where the sometime domesticated *C. frutescens* grows spontaneously or semi-wild. These three are known to grow in Africa, but only *C. annuum* var. *annuum* and *C. frutescens* are significant in India and the Far East. Virtually all of the capsicums that are found in markets around the world are *Capsicum annuum* var. *annuum*. The only way you can positively differentiate between the various *Capsicum* species is by the flower—corolla and calyx (see illustrations, pages 24–25).

Courtesy W. Hardy Eshbaugh

The flowers of *Capsicum baccatum* var. *pendulum* and *C. pubescens* are so different from the flowers of the other three species that if you saw those plants in bloom you would have no doubts. *C. baccatum* var. *pendulum* has a white flower with yellowish spots and white anthers that turn brownish yellow with age. *C. pubescens* has a beautiful purple flower with a tiny white border, and to make recognition even easier, its seeds are black. The flowers of the other three have white to greenish white petals and purple anthers. The flowers of *C. chinense* and *C. frutescens* are slightly greenish, while those of *C. annuum* var. *annuum* are milky white. Occasionally the annual pepper will have two flowers per node, but never more than two, so don't confuse it with *C. chinense*, which always has two or more, like cherries. Unless you are growing the plants yourself, you will probably not be confronted with this problem. Only *C. a.* var. *annuum* and *C. b.* var. *pendulum* have sweet varieties.

C. annuum var. *annuum* calyx

C. annuum var. *annuum* corolla

C. chinense calyx

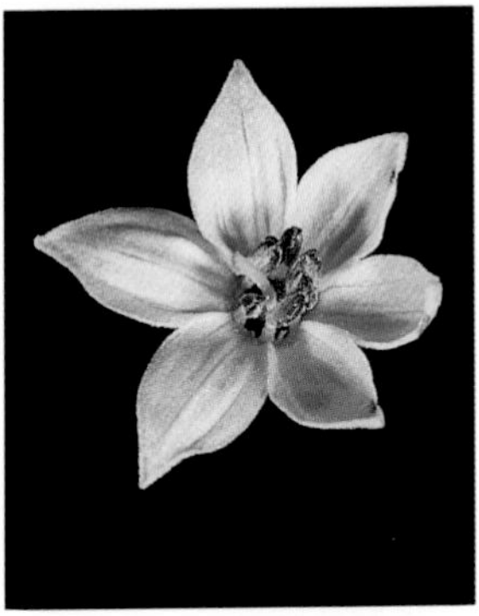

C. chinense corolla

C. frutescens calyx

C. frutescens corolla

C. baccatum var. *pendulum* calyx

C. baccatum var. *pendulum* corolla

C. pubescens calyx

C. pubescens corolla

For the most part, it is impossible to positively identify a species by the fruit alone. But don't worry—only three cultivars that are not *Capsicum annuum* var. *annuum* are grown commercially in the United States at this time: *C. frutescens* 'Tabasco' and *C. chinense*, the Dátil and Habanero. Your problem in the kitchen or market will be in distinguishing one *C. annuum* var. *annuum* cultivar from another.

WHAT KINDLES THE FLAME?

Capsaicin, the Pungent Principle

If you were to ask someone to name the one quality most peculiar to peppers, the response would probably be "they burn." The cause of the burning sensation is a potent, fat-soluble white crystalline compound named capsaicin (pronounced cap-say-i-sin) that is virtually insoluble in water, tasteless, and odorless. Capsaicin (CAPS) and its four principal derivatives make up the capsaicinoids, which occur only in capsicums and are stronger than the different pungent principles occurring in other piquant spices—ginger, horseradish, mustard, and black pepper. Three of these capsaicinoid components cause the sensation of "rapid bite" at the back of the palate and throat, and two others cause a long, low-intensity bite on the tongue and midpalate. Differences in the proportions of these compounds may account for the characteristic "burns" of the different capsicum cultivars. Pungency—sensory reaction to oral CAPS—is specific to sensory receptors for pain and temperature. It causes no reduction in the ability to detect physical stimuli—touch, sight, taste, smell, hearing. It should be considered as a gustatory trait along with sweet, sour, saline, bitter, salty, etc., instead of as spicy, sharp, caustic, acrid, biting, or other such unsatisfactory terms for its only quality.

In the mouth CAPS creates a sensation of warmth which increases to severe pain with large amounts. CAPS stimulates the sensory neurons in the mouth cavity and skin, causing them to produce the neuropeptide Substance P (SP), which delivers the message of pain to the brain. CAPS also has the ability to deplete SP from local sensory terminals in the skin, mucous membranes, and dental pulp with important therapeutic prospects. Only mammals have specific CAPS receptors on their sensory neurons; many other vertebrates, such as birds and frogs, lack similar receptors, hence are unaffected by CAPS.

A drop of a solution containing one part CAPS in 100,000 causes a persistent burning on the tongue. A drop of a solution of one part to a million imparts a perceptible warmth. The painfulness of the capsaicinoids is a self-limiting factor in their role as a human food constituent—you can eat just so much at "a sitting."

Since CAPS has virtually no flavor or odor, detection of it appears to be limited to feeling pain and/or heat. An oral method employing human "guinea pigs" as a taste panel, the Scoville Organoleptic Test of 1912, was the first means of analysis and is still used to express the amount of heat found in a pepper by modern methods. For example: the Bell group/type has zero Scoville heat units, while the Jalapeño and Cayenne may vary in heat from 2,500 to 25,000 units (usually 2,500 to 4,000); however, the Habanero rages in at 100,000 to 300,000 heat units.

Studies show that climatic conditions, variety, geographical location, stage of maturity, and location within the fruit influence CAPS content. Mature fruits have 50 percent more pungency than immature green ones. High night temperatures make for high CAPS. The majority of CAPS is in the placental partition (cross wall/veins) of the fruit. Seeds can acquire a degree of pungency through contact with the placenta. The glands which produce CAPS are found only in the placental tissue at its juncture with the cross walls and throughout the cross walls (veins, dissepiment).

CAPS increases the flow of saliva and tears and stimulates the mucous membranes of the nose, mouth, throat, and gastrointestinal tract. These functions work together to aid the digestion of food. The increased saliva helps ease the passage of food through the mouth to the stomach, where it is mixed with the activated gastric juice. These functions play an important role in the lives of people whose daily diet is principally starch-based.

However, these effects are produced only when the capsaicinoids in chillies contact the receptors directly and not when they are encapsulated; nor are such effects produced by material absorbed in the intestinal tract and carried by the bloodstream. Among CAPS' other effects are increasing fibrinolytic activity in the bloodstream, sweating, coughing, raising the metabolic rate, and some psychological stimulation. The outcomes of ingestion or topical application of chillies at low levels are considered significant and useful in preventative treatment, therapy, and as a research tool—far outweighing the burning pain that goes with eating or handling them.

Eating CAPS also causes the neck, face, and front of the chest to sweat in a reflexive response to the burning in the mouth. Very little CAPS is absorbed as it passes through the digestive tract, an uncomfortable consequence of which is jalaproctitis (burning defecation). If stomach ulcers are present or developing, the stimulation of gastric acid secretions caused by eating chillies is a potential discomfort, but chillies do not cause the ulcers.

How to Put Out the Fire

CAUTIONS AND PRECAUTIONS

Don't give up—you can put out the fire. CAPS is not soluble in water. No amount of water will wash it away, but cold water will give temporary relief by changing the surface temperature. In 1984 I discovered that washing one's hands in water containing a small amount of chlorine or ammonia stopped the burning. The chlorine or ammonia changes the CAPS into a water-soluble salt. This works wonders on hands, but of course you can't use chlorine or ammonia in your mouth. Like many organic compounds, CAPS is soluble in alcohol. Again this works on the skin, but caution is necessary when you drink it because alcohol breaks the natural barriers protecting the lining of your stomach—as well as being intoxicating. For your burning mouth, try cheap vodka as a mouthwash and gargle, then spit it out—great for the designated driver. Although CAPS is said to be fat-soluble, it takes a VERY long time for it to go into solution with fatty substances such as oil, butter, or shortening . . . too long when your mouth is on fire!

Your flaming mouth can also be relieved by lipoproteins such as casein which remove CAPS in a manner similar to the action of a detergent, breaking the bond the CAPS has formed with the pain receptors in your mouth. Yogurt, milk, and ice cream are the most readily available sources of casein. It is the casein, not the fat, in milk that does the job. Cheese and butter will not work. Generations of Indians have cooled fiery curries with raita, the traditional yogurt and chopped vegetable accompaniment to pepper dishes, but plain low-fat yogurt will do.

Emotional upsets, nicotine, or caffeine greatly increase the amount of acid in the stomach, and ulcers are often the result. It is only common sense to recognize that eating stimulating chillies while emotionally distressed, smoking, drinking coffee, or sipping margaritas will really fill your stomach with acid. The good news is that your body has a complex physical-chemical barrier to protect the stomach lining from the acid. The bad news is that aspirin and alcohol will readily invade that barrier. One aspirin causes the loss of only a small amount of blood, but in conjunction with alcohol it can cause excessive bleeding. Although the CAPS in chillies is harmless, in combination with nicotine, alcohol, aspirin, or coffee it may create more gastric acid than a body can bear—especially if you already have an ulcer.

Pungency Ratings/Heat Scale

	Scoville Units	*Pungency*	*Pepper Types*
0	0	Not pungent	Bells, Banana, Cherry, Cubanelle, Pimento, Romanian
1	100–500	Low	Ají Flor, Anaheim, Pepperoncini, Rocotillo, Tomato pepper
2	500–1,000		New Mexican Chile (variable according to cultivars, some more pungent)
3	1,000–1,500		Ancho, Mexi-Bell, Mulato, New Mexican Chile, Pasilla, Poblano
4	1,500–2,500		Cascabel, Chilaca, Hot Cherry
5	2,500–5,000	Intermediate	Cascabella, Guajillo, Hungarian Wax, Jalapeño, Mirasol, Peter pepper, Turkish
6	5,000–15,000		Romesco, Santa Fe Grande
7	15,000–30,000		High Cascabella, Catarina, De Arbol, Japonés, Serrano
8	30,000–50,000		Andean Ají, Cayenne, Costeño
9	50,000–100,000		Ají Amarillo, Ají Limón, Ají Oro, Chiltepín, Cusqueño, Dátil, Puca-uchu, Tabasco, Thai
10	100,000+	Very high	Habanero, Scotch Bonnet, West Indian Hot

If your passion is salsa picante and margaritas or some other alcoholic beverage, there is a safeguard you can take. Carbohydrates and proteins are digested more readily than fats. Stimulants such as alcohol take longer to attack someone whose stomach lining is coated with fat. If you have a tricky stomach, eat some cheese and/or cream before indulging in food highly seasoned with chillies and washed down with wine, beer, or margaritas.

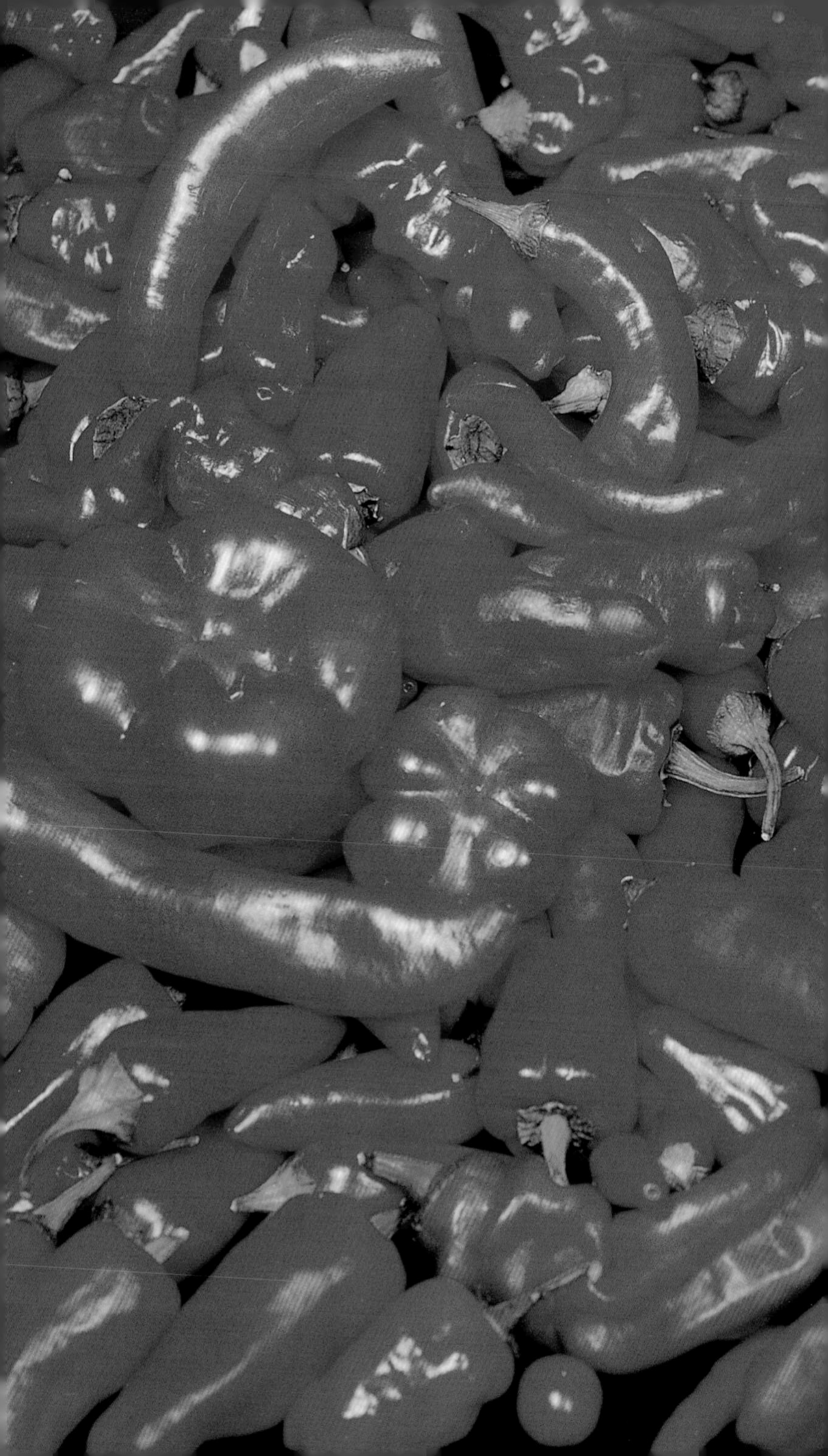

LOOK GOOD, SMELL GOOD, TASTE GOOD!

Color, Aroma, and Flavor

All capsicums are edible, but, like the Orwellian pigs, some are more edible than others. Flavor makes the difference. The flavor compound of capsicums is located in the outer wall (pericarp); very little is found in the placenta and cross wall (see Illustrated Glossary, Fig. 1) and essentially none in the seeds. Strong color and strong flavor go hand in hand because the flavoring principle appears to be associated with the carotenoid pigment. For example, the red Bell peppers are more flavorful than the less expensive, unripe greens. There is also a linkage to species—*Capsicum pubescens* (Rocoto) and the various varieties of *C. chinense* (Habanero) are more aromatic and have a decidedly different flavor than the varieties of *C. annuum* var. *annuum* (Bell pepper and Jalapeño), but most Anglo-Saxons find them too pungent to enjoy. Take a whiff and compare.

As in a painting, color in peppers is a most compelling element. Few foods are more exciting to our visual sense than an array of brilliant red, yellow, green, orange, purple, and brown capsicums. The carotenoid pigments responsible for the color in capsicums make them commercially important as natural dyes in food and drug products throughout the world. Red capsanthin, the most important pigment, is not found in immature, green capsicums. All capsicums change color as they mature from green to other hues. Color continues to develop for six weeks after the fully mature fruit is harvested. When the color of dried peppers fades, the flavor also fades. The distinctive *Capsicum* flavor develops only as the fruit ripens, reaching its peak at maturity.

Taste and smell/aroma are separate perceptions. Americans are beginning to appreciate aroma in capsicums as Mexicans, Asians, and Africans have long done. Several aroma compounds located in the outer wall or in the cross walls/veins produce the fragrance. The more delicate flavors of foods are recognized as aromas in the nasal cavity adjacent to the mouth by sensory cells much more discerning than those in the mouth. The taste buds on the tongue can discern certain flavors at dilutions up to one part in two million but odors can be detected at a dilution of one part in one billion. Awesome! Unfortunately, most of the fruity aroma is lost in processing.

PEPPERS ARE GOOD FOR YOU!

Nutritional Value

Peppers are extremely significant sources of many essential nutrients and are far richer in vitamins C and A than the usual recommended sources—citrus and carrots. The first pure vitamin C was produced from *Capsicum* peppers.

Vitamin C, the lack of which causes the dreaded disease scurvy, can be found only in fresh fruits and vegetables. Vitamin C is promptly destroyed by contact with oxygen and heat. The ascorbic acid content of peppers is highly variable, being affected by the type of soil, weather conditions, and maturity of the pod; nevertheless, peppers are still the richest source of vitamin C in the plant kingdom. The maximum is reached 35 to 49 days from fruit set, decreasing gradually with maturity.

Ripe capsicums are also a rich source of vitamin A. Vitamin A is formed from carotene and cryptoxanthin. Peppers have more than three times as much vitamin A as carrots, long held to be the food highest in that vitamin. Vitamin A increases as the pepper matures and dries. It is not lost when exposed to oxygen and is quite stable during the cooking and preservation process.

Capsicums are not only good, but good for you. Nutritionally, capsicums are a dietary plus. One Jalapeño contains more vitamin A and C than three medium-size oranges. Capsicums also contain significant amounts of magnesium, iron, thiamine, riboflavin, and niacin. Even though chillies are not usually eaten in large quantities, small amounts are important where traditional diets provide only marginal vitamins.

Since vitamin C is an unstable nutrient, readily destroyed by exposure to oxygen in the air, by drying, and by heating, and is soluble in water, keep cut or peeled capsicums well covered to prevent contact with oxygen and don't allow them to stand in water for more than one hour.

In this age of low calories, no fat, no salt, no cholesterol, etc., etc., capsicums conform to these food restrictions and at the same time enhance flavor and pep up otherwise bland creamless, butterless, eggless, saltless meals. Capsicums are a real health food!

LET'S CHOOSE 'EM AND USE 'EM!

Selection and Storage

Selection

FRESH

Capsicums are fruits that are used as a vegetable. Capsicums of any category can be picked when they are unripe (green, yellow, orange, white) or when a fully mature red, orange, yellow, purple, or brown. The compounds that furnish the flavor and the pungency of peppers do not develop immediately, but increase gradually with maturity. Consequently, the green fruits are less pungent and flavorful than the fully mature ones.

Choose fruits which have smooth, glossy skins and are firm to the touch. Peppers are a seasonal crop, and the best selection will be in the summer and fall. In the supermarket you are often met with a bin of peppers that are wrinkled has-beens—pick those with the fewest wrinkles. Remember to buy them in season, when they are bright, shiny, crisp, and less expensive, to freeze for later use.

DRIED

Not all peppers will air-dry or sun-dry satisfactorily. Those that dry well have thinner skins than the succulent ones such as the Bell pepper and Jalapeño. If possible, select dried peppers that are not packaged because you can select the better ones. Look for those that are clean, still pliable, not brittle, and bug-free (tiny holes in the skin are made by insects; also, powdery dust may be a sign that insects have been present). There should be no light-colored blotches or transparent spots (not to be confused with translucence, which is normal in several of the thin-skinned cultivars). Many packaged dried peppers are tagged with incorrect names. Pay no attention to those labels, but do look at the size, shape, and color and determine the variety for yourself by comparing with the photographs in this book.

Storage

If fresh peppers are not to be used immediately, they may be stored in the refrigerator for four or more weeks in the following manner. First, dry the pods; then place them in an airtight container designed so that you can remove the air, such as a Vacu Product jar, or a *tightly* sealed heavy, zip-lock plastic bag from which you have expelled all air by vacuum sealing or by drawing it out with a straw or tube; then store in the refrigerator. Each time you take peppers from the container, dry the unused pods and remove the air before resealing. If you cannot store them this way and are not going to use them within a week, it is best to freeze them to use for cooking. The key is to remove as much oxygen as possible, then keep them cool and dry. If you are in a hurry and plan to use the peppers within a week, put them in a paper bag—not plastic—and refrigerate.

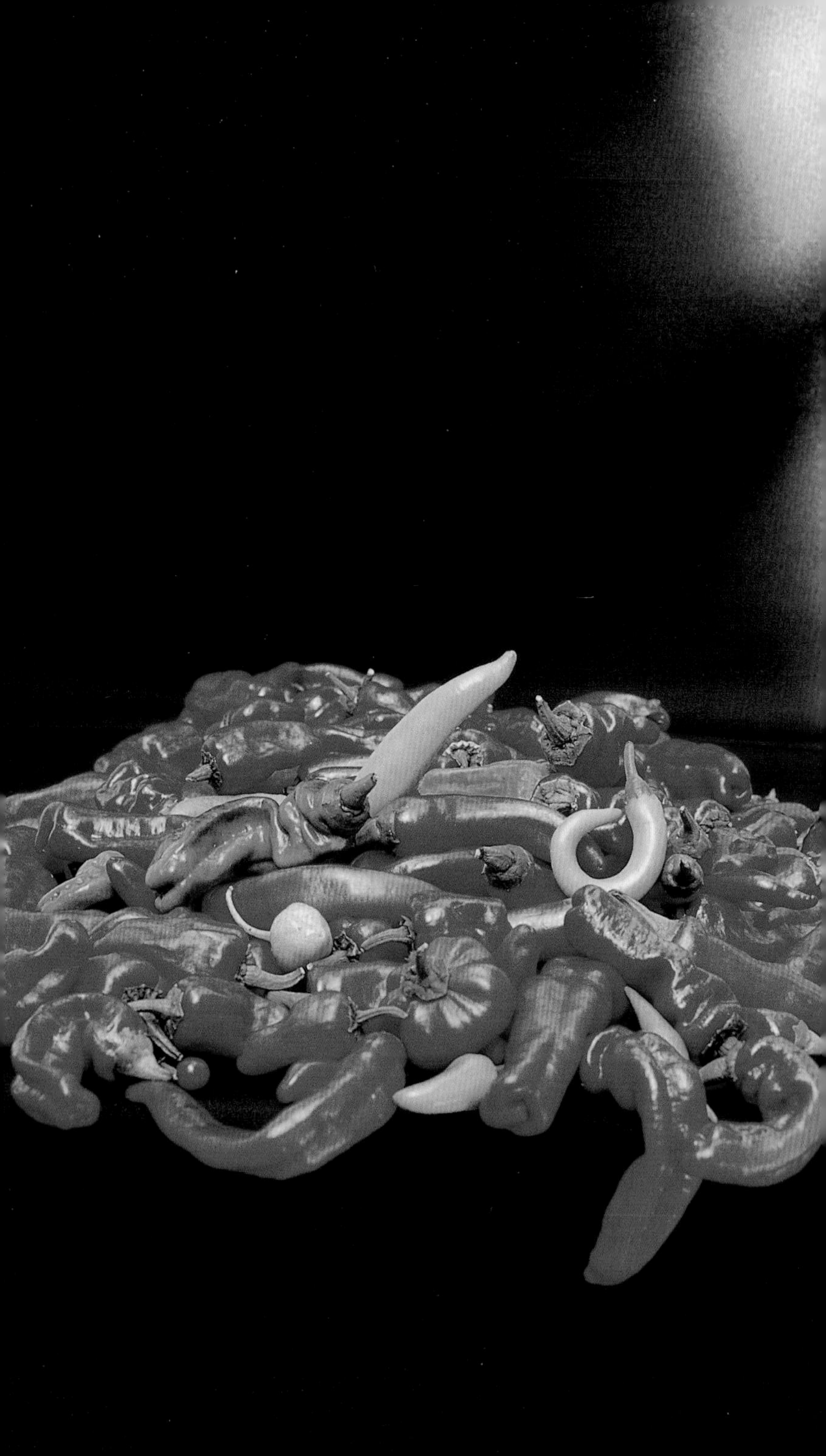

READY, SET, GO!

How to Roast and Rehydrate

Usually, if a recipe calls for a pepper to be roasted, it is done not only to remove the peel but also because that charred flavor is desired. Peppers can be "blistered" by one of several methods.

Blister Methods for Peeling

Step 1:
Before blistering the skin, always pierce or make a tiny slit in the pod to vent it so that it will not explode.

Burner roasting.
Place a cake rack, a hardware cloth, a steel cooling rack, or one of the new stove burner racks designed for stove-top grilling over the burner. Set the electric burner on high, or the gas burner on medium. Use kitchen tongs to rotate the pods. Continue turning until the entire pepper is blackened and blistered. Remove immediately to prevent cooking.

Broiler.
Arrange the peppers on an aluminum-foil-covered broiler pan or cookie sheet and place it 3 to 5

inches under the broiler. Turn the pods until completely charred. The peppers cook more by this method because the oven holds the heat. Do not use this method if shape and firmness are required in your peeled pepper. A number of pods can be charred quickly at the same time for making stews and sauces. Constant attention is required.

Oven roasting.
Preheat the oven to 550° F (280° C). Place the peppers on the oven rack and roast until blistered, 3 to 7 minutes. No turning is required.

Miscellaneous methods.
The same principles as explained above can be used with a charcoal or barbecue grill, or in a heavy griddle or skillet on top of the stove. Commercial roasters using revolving cylindrical cages set over gas flames have become commonplace in New Mexico and parts of the Southwest.

Step 2:
Remove the blistered pod from the heat and cool immediately in one of the following ways:

1. Place in a plastic or paper bag for 10 to 15 minutes.

2. Wrap in a cold, wet cloth and allow to steam 10 to 15 minutes.

3. Plunge into iced water. This method will result in a crisper pepper because it stops the cooking process immediately.

Step 3:
When the peppers are cool, begin peeling at the stem end with a small knife while holding the pod under running water. Wear rubber or disposable plastic gloves to protect sensitive hands. Keep chlorine water handy.

Step 4:
Slit the pod; remove the veins and seeds by cutting and washing. For stuffed chillies, leave the stems attached.

Freezing

Frozen peppers may be used in cooking or as stuffed peppers; they are too soft for salads. Leave the blistered and steamed peel on the pods before freezing to guard against loss of nutrients and flavor.

FOR NEW MEXICAN CHILES AND POBLANOS

1. Blister and steam but do not peel. When thawed, the skin comes off readily.

2. If space is a problem, remove the stem and seeds; otherwise, freeze the entire pod to prevent exposure to oxygen.

3. Flatten the whole pods to remove air and fold once for easy packing.

4. Pack in a moisture-vapor-proof package, excluding as much air as possible. Waterproof paper or plastic between the pods will facilitate separation.

FOR BELL PEPPERS AND LARGE SWEET PEPPERS

1. Wash, core, seed, and dry the peppers. Cut in half; place the halves on a metal pan or baking sheet and freeze.

2. Stack the frozen halves one inside the other and pack in a moisture-vapor-proof package, excluding as much air as possible. Freeze. Use from the bag as needed.

FOR CHILLIES (JALAPEÑOS, SERRANOS, ETC.)

1. Wash and dry the peppers. Place the whole pods on a metal pan or baking sheet and freeze.

2. Place the frozen pods in a moisture-vapor-proof package, excluding as much air as possible. Freeze. Use from the bag as needed.

Rehydration

Unless your dried peppers are going to be ground as flakes or powder, Anchos, Pasillas, Mulatos, Guajillos, Cascabels, Chipotles, and other dried peppers are usually rehydrated (plumped with water) before being used in food preparation. To do this, either place the chillies in a pan, cover with water, bring to a boil, remove from the heat, and let stand for an hour, or place in a bowl, cover with boiling water, and let stand for an hour. Drain the chillies and reserve the soaking water for use in sauces, soups, stews, etc. In order to retain the flavor and nutrients, do not leave the peppers in the water for more than an hour. After they have been drained, remove the stems, seeds, and veins. Now they are ready to be used as they are, shredded, chopped, or pureed with some of the soaking water to make a paste. The paste-like puree can be cooked in hot oil with other ingredients specified in the recipe to make a sauce. It keeps well in a covered jar in the refrigerator. For a richer flavor, the dried peppers can be toasted before rehydration.

Toasting Dried Chillies

Rinse the chillies under cold running water and pat dry. Heat a heavy skillet over medium-high heat until a drop of water will sizzle. Place a few chillies in the skillet and roast until just fragrant, turning frequently to avoid scorching. Large types, such as the Ancho, should be pliable; if they aren't, soak them in a bowl of boiling water for a few minutes. After soaking, remove the seeds and veins from the larger types, but this is not necessary for small ones. Rehydrate the toasted peppers as directed in the paragraph above.

HOW TO GET RICH QUICK!

Culture

Grow pungent peppers! The national average yield for cotton is 542 pounds an acre, earning around $208.40. Wheat averages 35.8 bushels per acre; at $1.62 a bushel, the value of an acre of wheat is $131.39. In the Rio Grande Valley of Texas, machine-picked Jalapeños yield 12 tons per acre at $0.28 per pound in the field, which is over $6,000 per acre. Small yellow wax types earn more than that, while the tiny Chiltepín will bring $10,000 per acre to the farmer who can find means to pick them. The only crops that bring more are marijuana and poppies. Notwithstanding, there are a couple of catches. One involves marketing, because a few pungent pods go a long way when used as food for humans, and the other is getting the little jewels picked. Caution: have a market before you plant!

In your home garden, allow three to four plants per person. Start the plants by sowing the seeds in shallow flats. Cover very lightly, moisten, and wrap in plastic to prevent drying. Keep indoors in a warm place. As soon as the seeds sprout, remove the plastic and place the flat under fluorescent lights or grow-lights until leaves are formed.

When the true leaves are well formed, transplant the seedlings into plastic or styrofoam transplanting trays. Lift the seedlings by the leaves. Grow them at 21° C (69.8° F), being careful that night temperatures do not fall below 17° C (62.6° F). To prevent "leggy" stems from developing, keep fluorescent lights or special grow-lights on for ten to twelve hours a day at approximately 10.2 cm (4 in.) to 2 feet from the plants, depending on the number of lights available, from the moment the radicle appears. After the plants attain a height of 12–15 cm (4¾–6 in.) and all danger of frost is past, plant them deeply in easily crumbled soil. This task should be performed in the early morning when the soil is cool but not below 13° C (55.5° F). Pepper roots will not grow and may be damaged if planted in soils having a lower temperature. If your soil thermometer reads above 13° C at the transplanting depth for three consecutive days, set out the plants. Space plants 31 cm. (12 in.) apart in rows 77–103 cm. (30–40 in.) apart. Close spacing results in more but smaller fruit. Add a cup of water to the hole, then transplant and cover with soil; irrigate immediately.

When direct planting, plant the seed in the moist soil on one side of the bed, near the furrow, at a depth of 6.4–12.5 mm (¼ to ½ in.). Transplanted plants bear earlier and produce a higher yield than field-planted peppers.

Plant peppers in full sun in a fertile, well-drained soil. About a week before transplanting, add 5 to 8 pounds of P_2O_5 fertilizer per 500 square feet, mixing it into the soil directly below the plants. A light or sandy soil will require nearly twice as much fertilizer. After the first blooms appear, apply ¼ to ½ cup of a high nitrogen fertilizer (21-0-0) as a side-dressing 35 to 40 cm (13¾ to 15¾ in.) from the plant's stem. Additional side-dressings should be made at about three-week intervals. Adequate moisture and good drainage are essential. Single rows on beds 30 inches apart should run in the direction of prevailing winds and/or north and south for better sunlight, pollination, aeration, and root orientation.

Pests and Controls

WEEDS

In the past, weed control was dependent on hand labor by "hoe hands." Today this kind of labor is not only costly but also difficult to come by, especially in the United States. A number of excellent herbicides have been developed to control weeds, but be certain to select one cleared for peppers—e.g., Devrinol. Apply the herbicide on top of shaped beds one day before planting and immediately mix it into the soil 3 inches deep. Plastic mulch with trickle irrigation is a weed control method that is rapidly increasing worldwide, and should comply with organic growing methods.

INSECTS

A variety of insect pests may damage peppers during the growing season. The best management practice is early detection of infestations and continued checking of the plants several times a week. The *Georgia Pest Control Handbook* from the Cooperative Extension Service of the University of Georgia College of Agriculture will help you if you want to select the proper insecticide.

Diseases and Control

Pepper breeders are busy developing and improving pepper varieties with the best line of control—genetic disease resistance—built in so that growers use as few chemicals as possible. The prevention and/or control of the several diseases that reduce quality and yield of fruit is critical in pepper production. Select seed of disease-resistant varieties. *Pepper Diseases: A Field Guide,* by Lowell Black et al. (Taipei: Asian Vegetable Research and Development Center, 1993), is a handy field guide to pepper diseases, available in both English and Spanish.

Curious Happenings

The unusual appearance at different stages in the development of various peppers causes both amazement and amusement, even inspiring the names of diverse cultivars such as "Peter/Penis Pepper." Although the developmental stages such as seen in the pictured Andean Ají, a *Capsicum baccatum* var. *pendulum*, occur in all species of *Capsicum*, some are more predisposed to the type of involution exhibited here than others, giving rise to unusual or abnormal forms. A latent predisposition manifests itself more often when the plant is grown under unfavorable conditions. When a particular developmental shape, color, flavor, size, etc., has appealed to humans, seed from specimens exhibiting the desired character have been selected for reproduction. If that character is genetically controlled and not just an environmental phenomenon, it becomes more predictable with constant and/or repeated selection for that particular character. As a result we have not only the Peter/Penis Pepper exhibiting unusual involution but also the Scotch Bonnet, Rocotillo, and others that turn inward at some point in their development instead of reaching the more usual extended shape, thereby producing a plethora of novel forms.

Another unusual situation is that of a normally sweet pepper variety producing a rogue pungent fruit on the same plant during the same growing season, much to the bewilderment of the gardener. Over time humans have selected for nonpungency, thereby producing the sweet varieties. However, the genes controlling the production of capsaicin, the pungent principle, were only suppressed. Adverse environmental conditions can activate those sleeping genes, causing them to "raise their ugly heads" again. Even if your sweet Bell Peppers cross pollinated with your Jalapeños, which can and does happen, that cross would not be expressed until you planted the resulting seed.

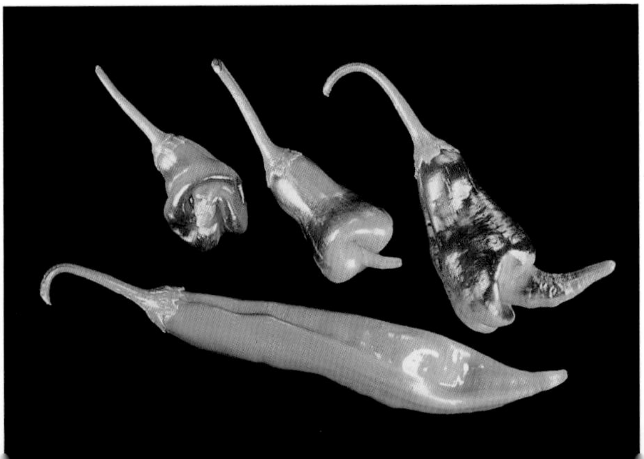

THE PEPPERS

Capsicum baccatum var. *pendulum*

Ají Flor (Flower), fresh

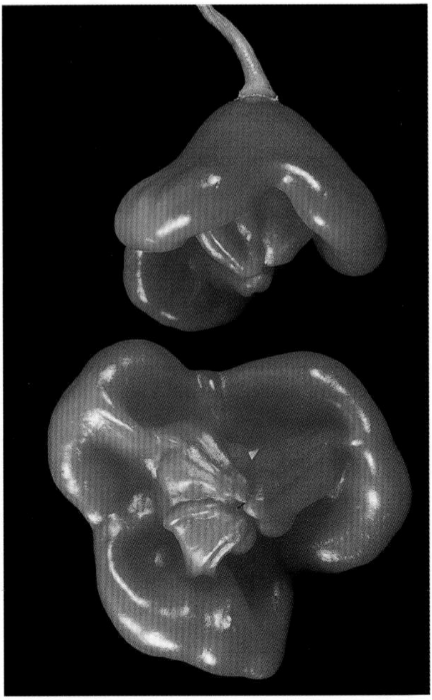

SIZE 1½ to 2 inches (3.8 to 5.1 cm) long; 1 to 2½ inches (2.5 to 6.4 cm) wide.

COLOR Yellow-green to golden yellow to orange-red.

FRUIT SHAPE Campanulate with sunken apex; truncate at peduncle attachment; cross section very corrugated. Scotch Bonnet type.

FLESH Thick walled.

PUNGENCY Only a slight pungency at the base where the placenta is attached; 0 to 3.

SUBSTITUTES Red Bell pepper, Pimento pepper.

OTHER NAMES Common name in South America is unknown. Called by a variety of names in the USA such as Ají Orchid or Orchid pepper, including, but incorrectly, Rocotillo.

SOURCES FRESH: Home gardens; Sunset Farms, Lago Vista, Texas.
DRIED: Not commonly used dried because not available yet.
PREPARED: Not yet processed.
SEEDS: Specialty seed houses.

USES Garnishes, flower arrangements, salads, appetizers, sauces, stews, casserole dishes.

REMARKS This exotic beauty is but one of the many little known species of *Capsicum baccatum* var. *pendulum* which are relatively unknown beyond South America. They grow well in south and central Texas and also in Pennsylvania, where they are grown by William Woys Weaver. The Penn brothers at Sunset Farms received their seed from Brazil, where it is used fresh as we do the Bell pepper. They called it Orchid pepper due to its flower shape. It does look like a flower, but not an orchid. Hence, Ají Flor (flower) instead of orchid. This delightful crisp, sweet pepper is very flavorful and is now nose to nose with my 1984 favorite, Rocotillo. You'll love it.

Capsicum baccatum var. *pendulum*

Ají Limón, fresh and dried

SIZE 1 to 1¾ inches (2.5 to 4.5 cm) long; ⅜ to ¾ inches (1 to 1.9 cm) wide at shoulder.

COLOR Pale yellow-green to lemon yellow.

FRUIT SHAPE Elongate, flattened; wider at midpoint, tapering to an acutely pointed apex; obtuse at peduncle attachment; cross section with intermediate corrugations. Andean Ají type.

FLESH Thin walled.

PUNGENCY High; 7.

SUBSTITUTES Andean Ají, Dátil, Habanero, Santa Fe Grande/Caribe.

OTHER NAMES Its South American common names are unknown.

SOURCES FRESH: Home gardens, Sunset Farms.
DRIED: Sunset Farms.
PREPARED: Not processed commercially.
SEEDS: For now, friends.

USES With citrus fruits in sherbets, preserves, marmalades; salsas, salad dressings, chutneys, and stir fry dishes.

REMARKS A delicious lemon (*limón*) flavor which complements marmalades and chutneys. Try it in lemon or lime marmalade and in lemon butter for fish or vegetables. It is possible to dry this pepper at 374° F. (190° C.) in your oven or with a convection oven according to oven's printed directions. Recently introduced from Peruvian lowlands of South America.

Capsicum baccatum var. *pendulum*

Ají Oro, fresh

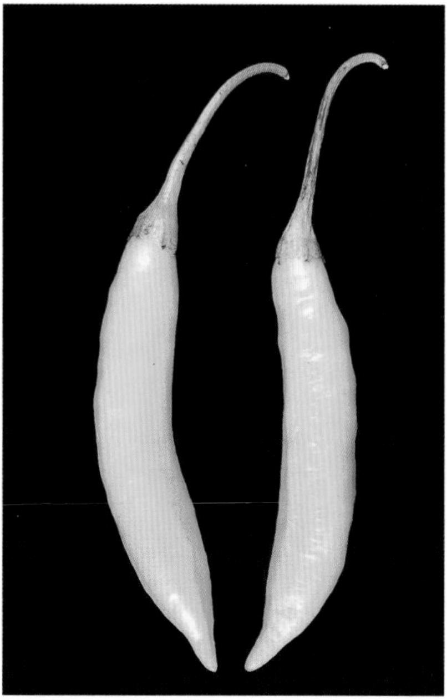

SIZE	3 inches (7.6 cm) long; ½ inch (1.3 cm) wide.
COLOR	Pale yellow-green to lemon yellow.
FRUIT SHAPE	Elongate cylinder, tapering to a pointed apex; obtuse at peduncle attachment; smooth cross section. Andean Ají type.
FLESH	Thin walled.
PUNGENCY	High; 7.
SUBSTITUTES	Andean Ají, Cayenne, De Arbol, Serrano, Thai.
OTHER NAMES	Ají Amarillo, Penn's Golden.
SOURCES	FRESH: Home gardens, specialty food stores. DRIED: Not available yet. PREPARED: Not processed commercially. SEEDS: Specialty seed catalogs; hard to find.
USES	Table sauces, tomato dishes, pasta dishes, soups, ceviche.
REMARKS	This golden pepper has a nice fresh flavor which can be used as you would the Serrano. It is the most pungent of the *Capsicum baccatum* var. *pendulum* cultivars which I yet know.

Capsicum baccatum var. *pendulum*

(Ají) Puca-uchu, fresh

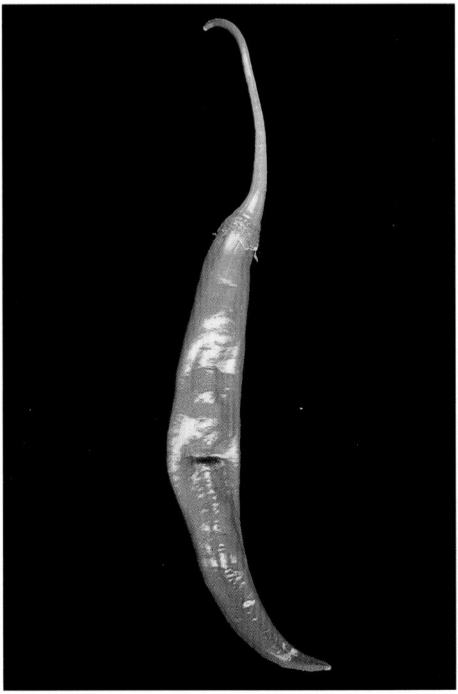

SIZE 2½ to 3 inches (6.4 to 7.6 cm) long; ⅝ to ¾ inch (1.6 to 1.9 cm) wide.

COLOR Green to orange to orangish red; glossy.

FRUIT SHAPE Elongate, tapering to a very sharp pointed apex; obtuse at peduncle attachment; cross section intermediate corrugations. Andean Ají type. (The type for the Andean Ají or any elongate *Capsicum baccatum* var. *pendulum*.)

FLESH Medium thick walled.

PUNGENCY High; 7 to 9.

SUBSTITUTES Cayenne, Serrano, Thai, any Andean Ají.

OTHER NAMES Cuerno de Oro; so little is known about the common names of South American peppers it is difficult to attach common names to them.

SOURCES FRESH: Home gardens, farmer's markets.
DRIED: Not available.
PREPARED: Not available in USA; sauces prepared commercially in South America.
SEEDS: Specialty seed catalogs; hard to find.

USES As you would a Serrano; table sauces, potato and cassava dishes, dips, ceviche.

REMARKS *Capsicum baccatum* var. *pendulum* is the only species of the domesticated capsicums which has not become well established beyond its place of origin in the southern Andes. It and the universal *Capsicum annuum* var. *annuum* are the only domesticated species to have cultivars which are not pungent such as Ají Flor and Bell. Today, it is cultivated in Argentina, Bolivia, Brazil, Costa Rica, Ecuador, and Peru. This South American pepper is a recent addition to the repertoire of North American peppers and is still hard to come by, but worth looking for.

Capsicum annuum var. *annuum*

Anaheim / New Mexican Chile, fresh and dried

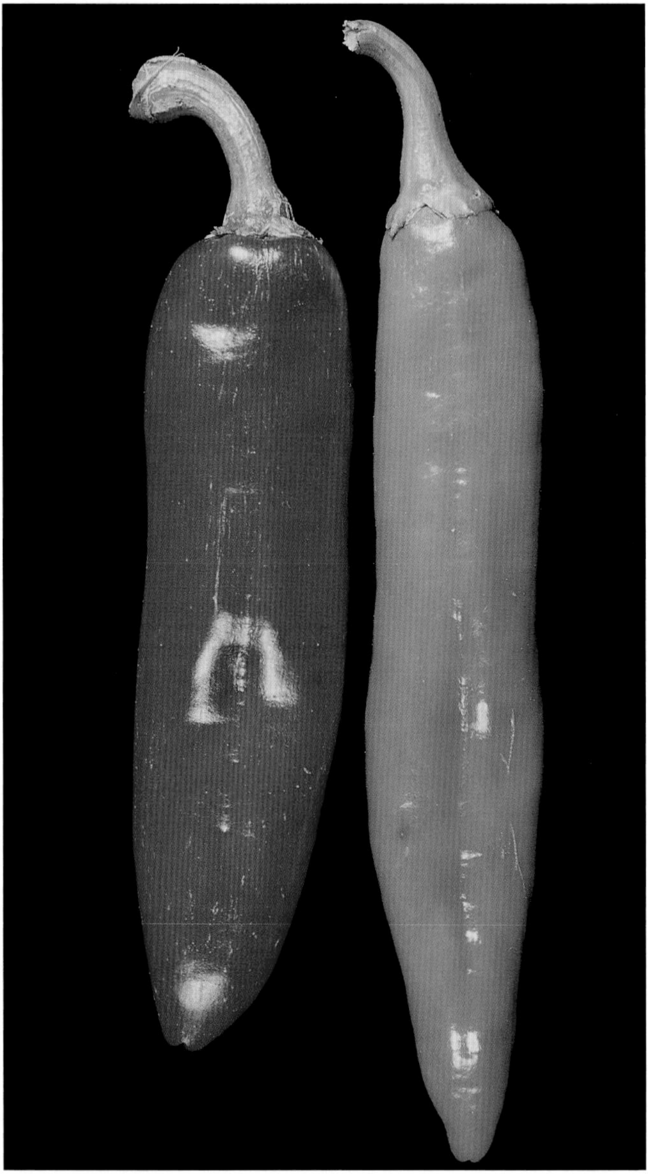

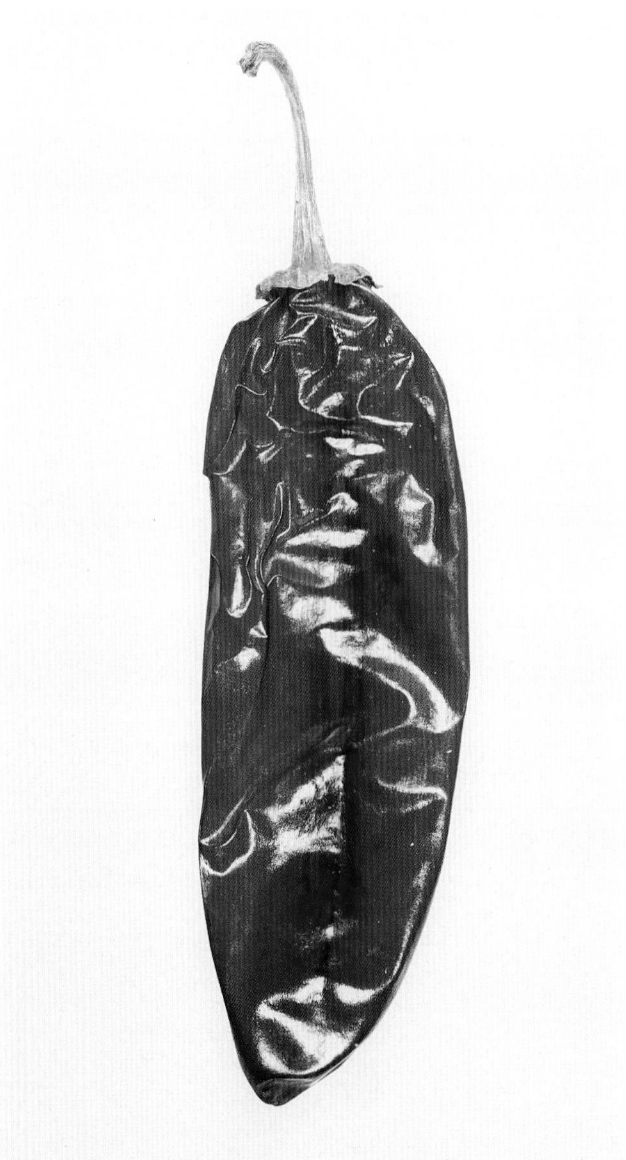

SIZE 7 to 10 inches (17.8 to 25.4 cm) long; 1 to 1¾ inches (2.5 to 4.5 cm) wide.

COLOR FRESH: Bright green to red.
DRIED: Brownish red.

FRUIT SHAPE Elongate, flattened, tapering to a blunt point at apex; obtuse at peduncle attachment; cross section slightly corrugated. Anaheim/New Mexican Chile type.

FLESH Medium thick walled.

PUNGENCY Low to intermediate depending on cultivar; 3 to 5.

SUBSTITUTES Poblano for fresh, Ancho or Guajillo for dried.

OTHER NAMES Anaheim, California Long Green Chile, Chilacate, Chile College, Chile Colorado, Chile de Ristra, Chile Verde, Chimayo, Hatch, Long Green/Red Chile, New Mexico 6-4, New Mexico No. 9, Pasado, and many other cultivars. Frequently packaged dried fruits are incorrectly labeled Guajillo.

SOURCES FRESH: Most food stores in the Southwest, but becoming more available throughout the country.
DRIED: Same as fresh.
PREPARED: In the spice section of food markets; sold as pizza pepper; red pepper flakes, powdered (sometimes as paprika and also in commercial chili powder), as well as pure; also sold as canned green chiles, whole or chopped.
SEEDS: Most seed suppliers will have one or more cultivars such as: Anaheim, Anaheim M, Anaheim TMR 23, Big Jim, California, Chimayo, Colorado, Coronado, Eclipse, Española Improved, New Mexico No. 9, NuMex, R-Naky, Red Chile, Sandia (pungent), Sunrise, Sunset, TAM Mex-6, TAM Mild Chile-1 and 2, TMR 23, etc.

USES FRESH GREEN: canned, fresh, frozen, or *pasado* (see page 89). Stuffed (*relleno*), in soups, stews, sauces, casseroles, fried, as a garnish, in soufflés, etc., as well as for decoration.
DRIED RED: cooked in stews, soups, sauces; as a table spice; in condiments; as decoration.

REMARKS This colorful pepper was developed from dried peppers brought from Mexico to New Mexico by Juan Oñate in 1597. The progenitor was said to be the Pasilla, probably the Pasilla de Oaxaca, not the Pasilla/Chilaca. Several centuries later, that New Mexican stock was taken to Anaheim, California, by Emilio Ortega and further developed before returning to the Southwest to become the symbol of the region and the keystone of Southwestern cookery. It is not used in traditional interior Mexican or Tex-Mex dishes.

Capsicum annuum var. *annuum*

Ancho, dried

SIZE	4 inches (10.2 cm) long; 2½ inches (6.4 cm) wide.
COLOR	Dark brown, brick red after soaking; sun dried are red, while gas dried are blacker; fresh Anchos are red when mature.
FRUIT SHAPE	Flattened, wrinkled; lobate at peduncle attachment; cross section with intermediate corrugations. Poblano type.
FLESH	Medium thick walled.
PUNGENCY	Low to intermediate; 3 to 5.
SUBSTITUTES	Mulato, Anaheim/New Mexican Chile (*chile colorado*), Pasilla.
OTHER NAMES	Chile Colorado (in Texas), Mulato, Pasilla.
SOURCES	FRESH: See Poblano. DRIED: Most food stores in the Southwest, ethnic specialty stores. PREPARED: Basis of commercial chili powder which is mixed with other peppers and spices; in spice section. SEEDS: Specialty seed suppliers. Available cultivars: Chorro, Esmeralda, Flor de Pabellón, Verdeño.
USES	In sauces for enchiladas, chili con carne, adobados (meat prepared with a sour seasoning paste is *adobado* or pickled), commercial chili powders.
REMARKS	The most used dried pepper in Mexico. Air-dried pods are more susceptible to insects than heat-dried pods. When soaked, the dried Ancho will turn brick red. The Ancho is the dried state of the varieties of Poblano which are red at maturity (See pages 132–134).

Capsicum annuum var. *annuum*

Banana Pepper (Not Pungent) and Hungarian Wax (Pungent), fresh

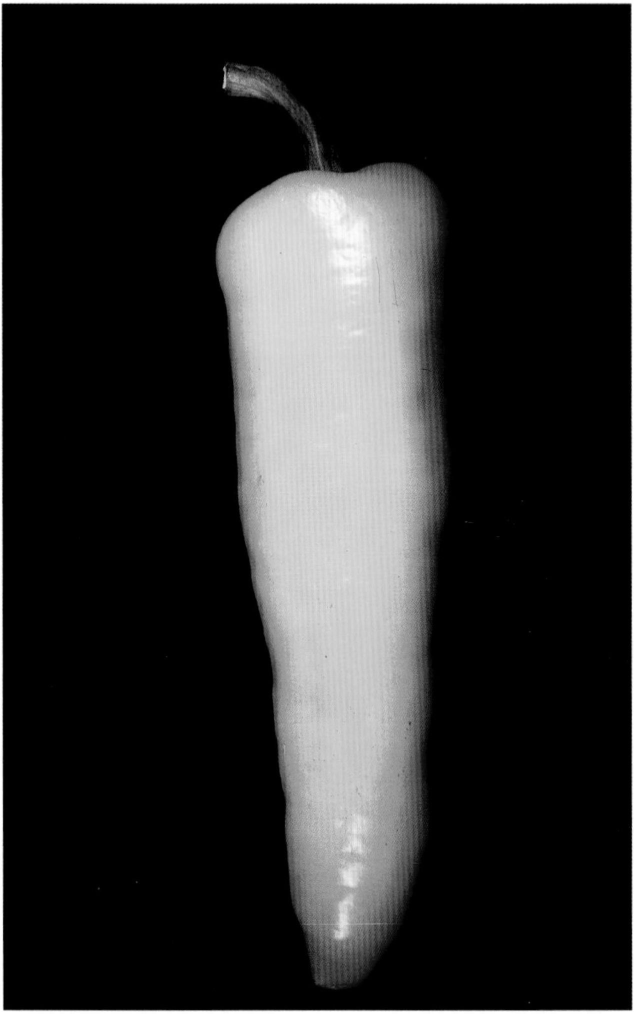

SIZE 5½ to 6 inches (14 to 15.2 cm) long; 1½ inches (3.8 cm) wide.

COLOR Pale yellow-green to yellow, maturing to bright red.

FRUIT SHAPE Elongated cylinder, tapering to a pointed apex; truncate peduncle attachment; cross section slightly corrugated. Long wax type.

FLESH Medium thick walled.

PUNGENCY Banana not pungent; Hungarian Wax pungent (more so when mature red); 0 to 7.

SUBSTITUTES Cubanelle for sweet; Caloro, Santa Fe Grande for pungent.

OTHER NAMES Hungarian Yellow Wax, Sweet Banana.

SOURCES FRESH: Home garden, farmer's markets.
DRIED: Not used dried.
PREPARED: Pickled Banana peppers available in food stores.
SEEDS: Most seed suppliers. Available cultivars: Early Sweet Banana, Giant Yellow Banana, Hungarian Yellow Wax, Long Sweet Yellow.

USES FRESH: in the yellow stage in salads, as garnishes, stuffed in raw celery, in vegetable dishes and stews, fried.
PICKLED: as garnishes, in salads, in sandwiches, as a condiment.

REMARKS Developed by Corneli Seed Company in 1940 from seed introduced to the United States from Hungary in 1932. Banana/Hungarian Wax peppers are used only in the yellow stage, not in the ripe red stage, although they are quite edible when ripe red. Easily grown but not often found fresh in the supermarkets.

Capsicum annuum var. *annuum*

Bell Pepper, fresh

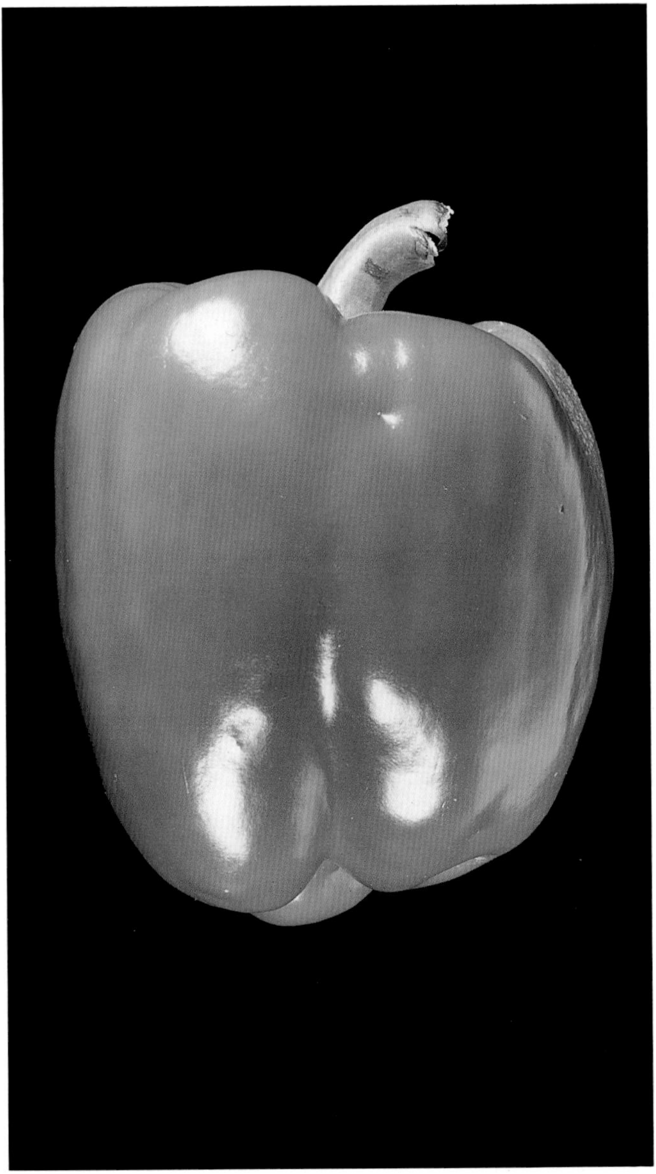

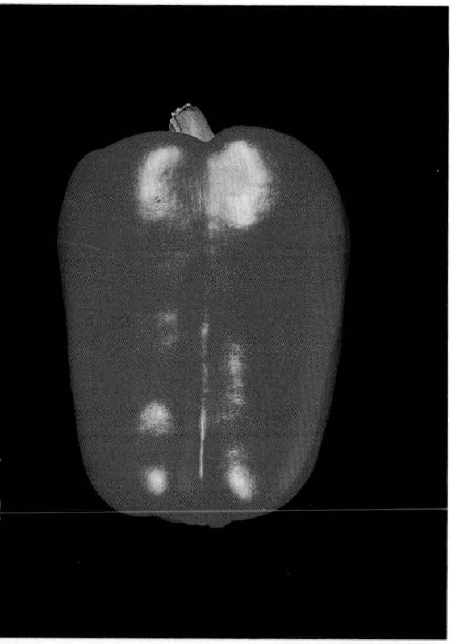

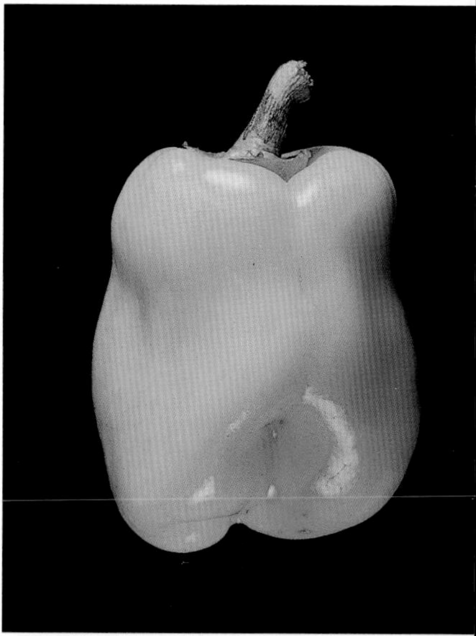

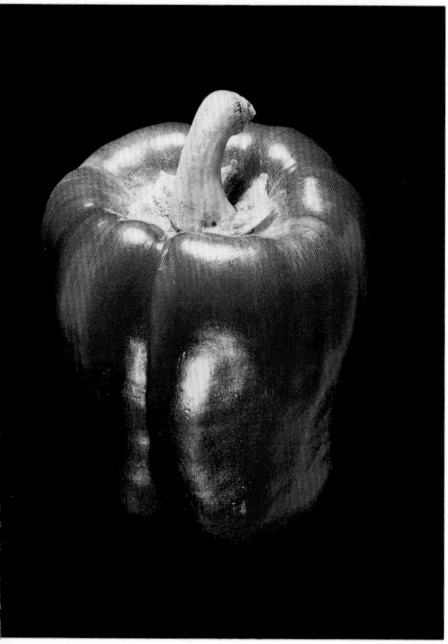

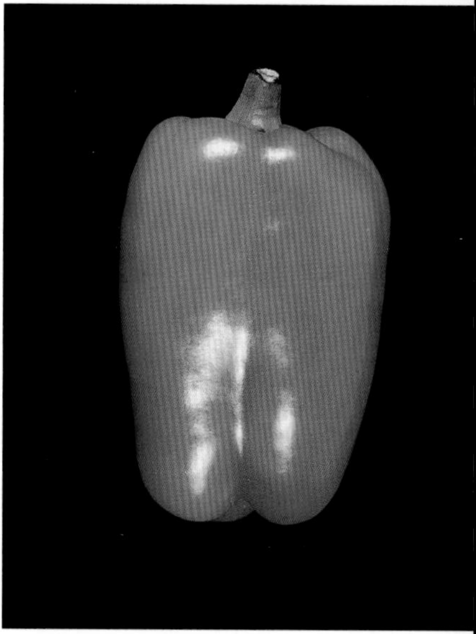

SIZE 4 to 6 inches (10.2 to 15.2 cm) long; 3½ to 4 inches (8.9 to 10.2 cm) wide.

COLOR Green to red, orange, yellow, brown, ivory, or purple.

FRUIT SHAPE Blocky; apex sunken; lobate at peduncle attachment; cross section deeply lobed. A few cultivars, such as the tomato-shaped Sunnybrook or the long, narrow Ruby King, do not conform. Bell pepper type.

FLESH Thick walled.

PUNGENCY Not pungent, except for Mexi-Bell; 0 to 5.

SUBSTITUTES Ají Flor, Banana, Cubanelle, Pimento/Pimiento, Tomato pepper.

OTHER NAMES Capsicum, Chile de Agua, Mango, Morrón, Pimentón, Pimiento, or any one of the hundreds of hybrid cultivar names.

SOURCES FRESH: Food stores, farmer's markets, home garden.

DRIED: Bell peppers are not dried whole. Dehydrated flakes can be found in the spice section of food stores.

PREPARED: Ripe red ones are canned as a pale substitute for Pimento.

SEEDS: There are a multitude of cultivars; any seed company will have one or more. Popular cultivars: Ace Hybrid, Argo, Big Bertha, Klondike Bell, Ma Belle, Oriole, Staddons Select, TAMBEL-1, 2, 3, and 4, Yolo Wonder.

USES Stuffed (parboil 2 to 3 minutes first), fried, in casseroles, vegetable dishes, salads, garnishes, relishes, soups, crudités, sauces.

REMARKS Bell peppers were recorded in 1681 from Panama. There are more than 200 registered cultivars to choose from. The mature red or colored fruit is much more flavorful and digestible than the common green ones. We have had to eat green Bell peppers in the past because they ship better and have a longer shelf life than the superior ripe ones. Dutch growers recently introduced the delicious colored ones to an American market which has a growing interest in better food. Demand forced American farmers to let some of their green peppers ripen to their full color before marketing. Add some red Bell peppers to pungent sauces and stews to enhance flavor.

Cascabel, fresh and dried

SIZE 1 to 1¾ inches (2.5 to 4.5 cm) long; 1 to 1½ inches (2.5 to 3.8 cm) wide.

COLOR FRESH: Dark green to reddish brown.
DRIED: Dark reddish brown with translucent, glossy skin.

FRUIT SHAPE Oblate, blossom end blunt; lobate at peduncle attachment; smooth cross section. The elongate Guajillo is often mislabeled as Cascabel because its dried seeds rattle. Look for the round shape. Cherry type.

FLESH Medium thick walled.

PUNGENCY Intermediate; 4 to 5.

SUBSTITUTES Catarina, Cayenne, Guajillo, Japonés.

OTHER NAMES Bolita, Bola, Chile Trompo, Coban, Trompillo.

SOURCES FRESH: Not used.
DRIED: Imported; Mexican food stores, border markets.
PREPARED: Probably not imported.
SEEDS: Mexico or specialty seed suppliers. Cultivars: Real Mirasol, Carricillo.

USES Ground/powdered in cooked sauces, tamales, sausages, casseroles, as a seasoning; toasted or untoasted; ground as paprika.

REMARKS Some of the dried seeds are often ground with the peppers in sauces where they impart a somewhat nutty flavor. The larger, elongate Guajillo is often mislabeled Cascabel. Look at the shape. Cascabel is always round—Guajillo, NEVER! The two do not have the same flavor or coloring power; however, the seeds rattle in both of them after drying.

Cascabella, fresh

SIZE 1¼ inches (3.2 cm) long; 1 inch (2.5 cm) wide.

COLOR Yellow to orange to vermilion.

FRUIT SHAPE Conical, tapering to a point; truncate at the peduncle attachment; smooth cross section. Small wax type.

FLESH Medium thick walled.

PUNGENCY Low to intermediate; 3 to 7.

SUBSTITUTES Caloro, Fresno, Hungarian Wax, Santa Fe Grande/Caribe.

OTHER NAMES None.

SOURCES FRESH: Home gardens, farmer's markets, occasional supermarket.
DRIED: Not dried.
PREPARED: Pickled in most supermarkets.
SEEDS: Some seed catalogs. Available cultivars: TAM Cascabella, TAM Rio Grande Gold Sweet.

USES The small, yellow fruit is highly desired for pickling.

REMARKS The name comes from two Spanish words—*cascara* (skin) and *bella* (beautiful). Although it sounds like *cascabel* (small bell), the words are unrelated. It closely resembles the larger Fresno. This yellow pepper is highly desired by pickle packers, but its small size makes picking difficult. Farmers who have a market before planting can get a big price for Cascabellas. In the past Floral Gem, a similar small, yellow, pungent pepper was also sought after for pickles. The latter differed from Cascabella by being slightly indented at the apex. Although Floral Gem was figured and described in *Peppers: The Domesticated Capsicums*, it has fallen into disfavor for some reason, and seeds are no longer available, having been supplanted by Cascabella.

Catarina, fresh and dried

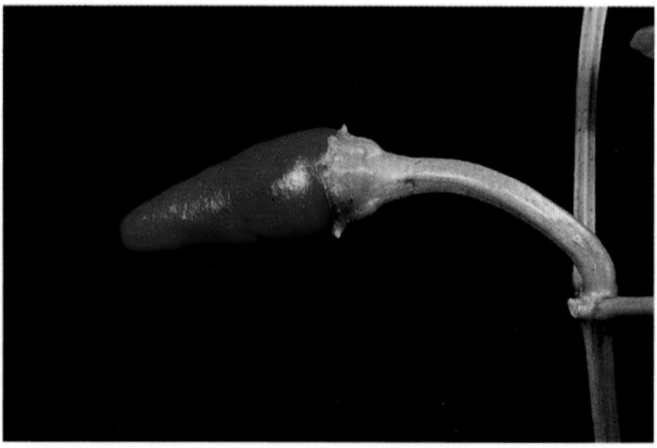

SIZE 1 to 1½ inches (2.5 to 3.8 cm) long; ½ inch (1.3 cm) wide.

COLOR Green to red.

FRUIT SHAPE Conical, tapering to a point; obtuse at the peduncle attachment; smooth cross section. Small hot type.

FLESH Thin walled.

PUNGENCY High to very, very high; 7 to 9.

SUBSTITUTES Cayenne, De Arbol, Guajillo, Japonés.

OTHER NAMES Cascabelillo, Mirasol.

SOURCES FRESH: Not often used fresh.
DRIED: Mexican border food stores.
PREPARED: Ground into powder at home.
SEEDS: Specialty seed catalogs, Mexico.

USES Seasoning for tamales, chili con carne, and Mexican dishes.

REMARKS Catarina is a small parakeet, or *catarinita*. The pepper is thought to be shaped like the beak of a parakeet. Dried, translucent red fruits allow the seeds to rattle. It is favored for tamales and can be used green in table sauces as is the Serrano.

Capsicum annuum var. *annuum*

Cayenne, fresh and dried

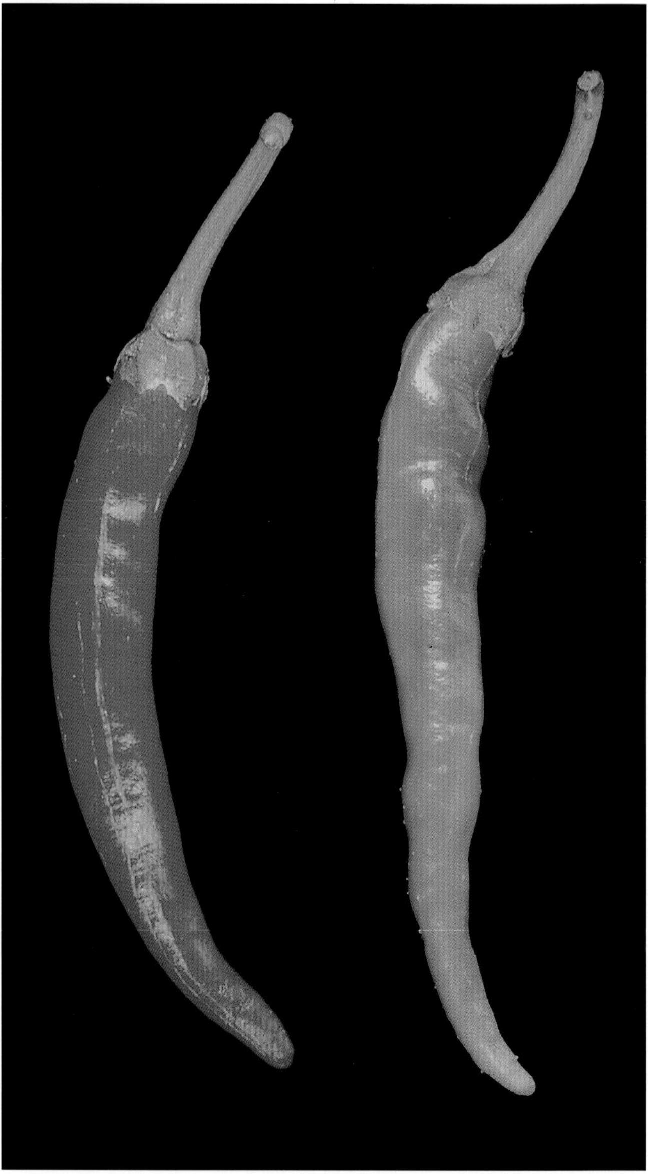

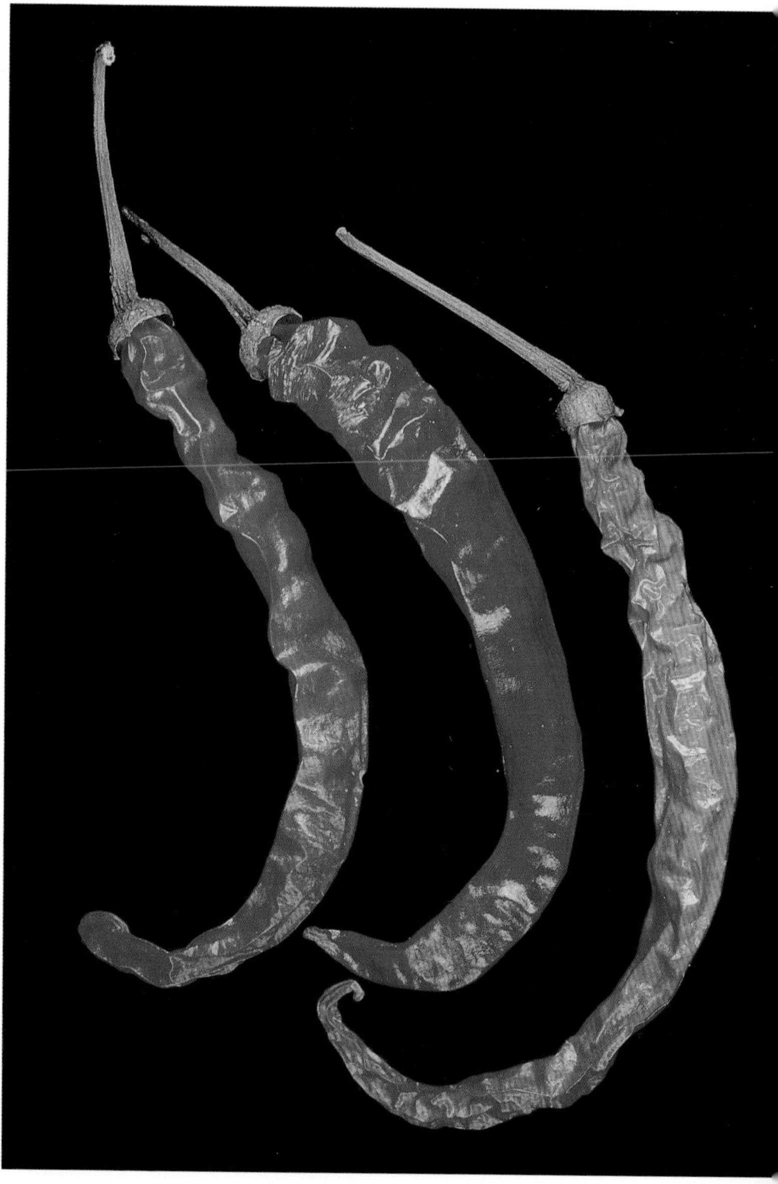

SIZE 5 to 6 inches (12.7 to 15.2 cm) long; ½ to ¾ inch (1.3 to 1.9 cm) wide.

COLOR Dark green to red.

FRUIT SHAPE Elongate cylinder, wrinkled, curved; pointed apex; obtuse at peduncle attachment; cross section with intermediate corrugations. Cayenne type.

FLESH Thin walled.

PUNGENCY High to very high; 7 to 9.

SUBSTITUTES Jalapeño, Serrano, Thai.

OTHER NAMES A pepper of the Cayenne type was one of the first capsicums introduced to the Far East. It has become the most common type of *Capsicum* grown in the world with different names in every country.

SOURCES FRESH: Farmer's markets, home gardens, and some food stores throughout the country.
DRIED: In any ethnic or supermarket spice section, powdered, dehydrated, or whole.
PREPARED: Packaged ground in the spice section of almost any food store as Red pepper or Cayenne pepper; canned sauces; used in take-out sauces; used in some Cajun seasonings.
SEEDS: Most seed suppliers carry one or more varieties. Available cultivars: Charleston Hot, Cayenne Langer, Cayenne Large Red Thick, Cayenne Pickling, Golden Cayenne Hades Hot, Hot Portugal, Japanese Fuschin, Jaune Long, Long Red, Long Slim, Mammoth Cayenne, Ring of Fire, TAM Cayenne-1.

USES In Creole and Cajun, Indian, Indonesian, Thai, Pakistani, Hunan, and Szechuan cookery. In meat and vegetable dishes, salad dressings, and as a table spice.

REMARKS Cayenne type peppers are the most used variety throughout the world because they were carried by the Portuguese to Africa, India, and the Far East early in the sixteenth century (see my book *Red Hot Peppers* [1993], pp. 13–19, and *Geographical Review* 83, no. 2 [1993]: 145–168). I have seen varieties of them in the Middle East, Far East, India, Indonesia, Tibet, Thailand, Japan, Central Asia—you name it. In those places they do not have a great variety of pepper types, but they do have plenty of what they have. Although Cayenne originated in Latin America, it is not grown there to any extent today. Cayenne pepper or powdered Cayenne can be used to upgrade the pungency of milder, more flavorful peppers and as a flavor enhancer in sauces, soups, salad dressings, etc.

Capsicum annuum var. *annuum*

Cherry, fresh

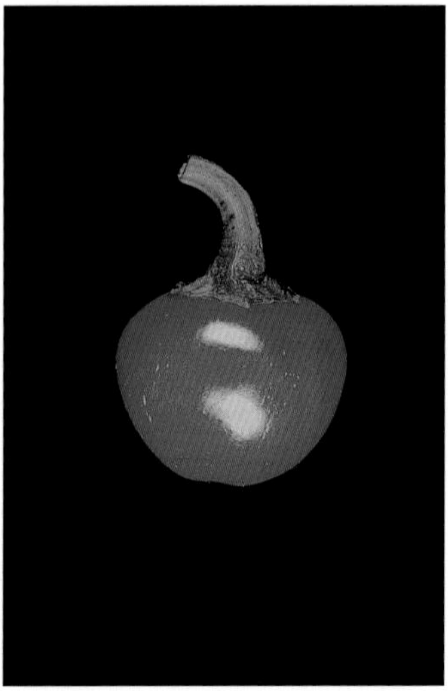

SIZE ¾ to 1 inch (1.9 to 2.5 cm) long; 1¼ to 1½ inches (3.2 to 3.8 cm) wide.

COLOR Medium green to red.

FRUIT SHAPE Oblate, blossom end blunt; cordate at peduncle attachment; smooth cross section. Cherry type.

FLESH Medium thick walled.

PUNGENCY Not pungent or low; 0 to 4.

SUBSTITUTES Any pickled pepper.

OTHER NAMES Hot Cherry, Hungarian Cherry, Sweet Cherry.

SOURCES FRESH: Home gardens, farmer's markets.
DRIED: Not used dried.
PREPARED: Pickle section in food markets.
SEEDS: Most seed suppliers have at least one cultivar. Available cultivars: Bird's Eye, Cerise, Cherry Jubilee, Cherry Sweet, Christmas Cherry, Super Sweet, Red Giant, Tom Thumb.

USES Pickles, relishes, jams, salads, garnishes, condiments.

REMARKS It must have been developed by pre-Columbian Indians because a Cherry type pepper was illustrated in a German herbal by Leonhart Fuchs in 1542, only fifty years after Columbus discovered peppers. It is a fairly common form in India, where peppers are eaten with every meal by virtually everyone.

Capsicum annuum var. *annuum*

Chilaca, fresh

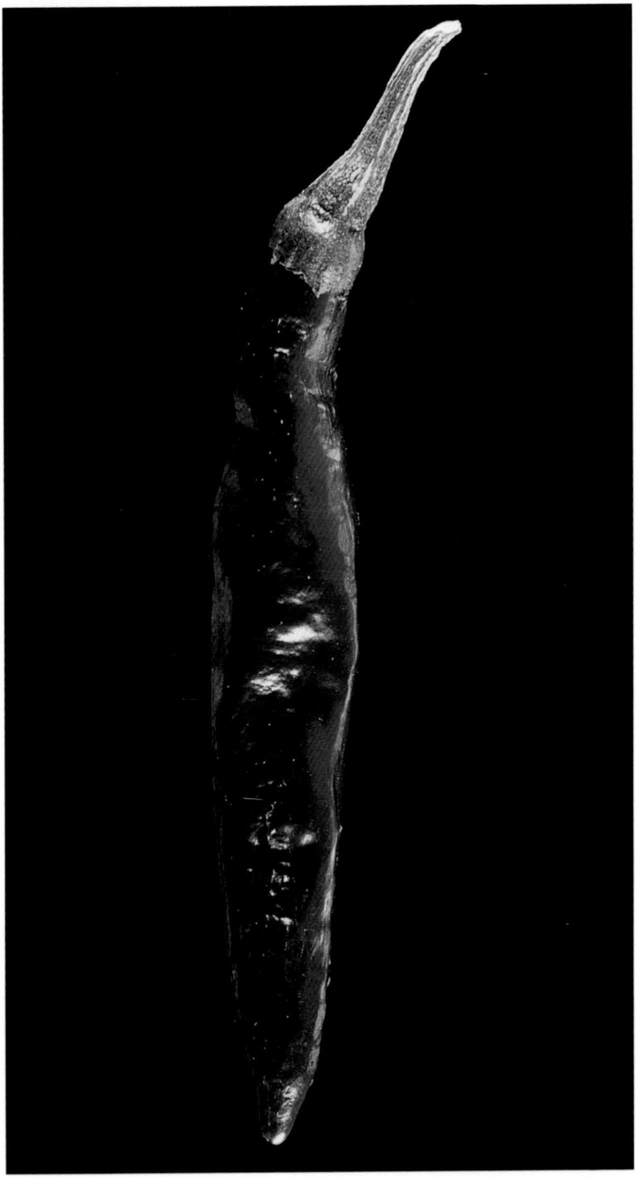

SIZE 6 to 12 inches (15.2 to 30.5 cm) long; 1¼ to 1½ inches (3.2 to 3.8 cm) wide.

COLOR Dark blackish green ripening to dark brown.

FRUIT SHAPE Elongate, flattened, irregular, wrinkled; pointed apex; obtuse at peduncle attachment; very corrugated cross section. Anaheim/New Mexican Chile type.

FLESH Medium thick walled.

PUNGENCY Low to intermediate; 3 to 5.

SUBSTITUTES FRESH: Poblano.

OTHER NAMES Pasilla.

SOURCES FRESH: Probably not found commercially outside Mexico; home gardens.
DRIED: Many supermarkets in the Southwest; some ethnic food stores.
PREPARED: Made into paste which is formed in small squares and dried. This is called *pasado* (spent or old).
SEEDS: Catalogs of specialty seed houses. Available cultivars: Apaseo and Pabellón 1.

USES Fresh in sauces and as a vegetable after roasting/charring and peeling; stir fry.

REMARKS Chilaca is the name of the fresh state of the Pasilla. In Mexico the names for the fresh and dried states are always distinct. This Mexican pepper has a flavor much like that of the Poblano. Its long, narrow shape precludes stuffing, but it can be sliced and chopped and used in any other way one would use the Poblano.

Capsicum annuum var. *annuum*

Chilcoztli, dried

SIZE 5 to 6½ inches (12.7 to 16.5 cm) long; ¾ to 1¼ inches (1.9 to 3.2 cm) wide.

COLOR Dark reddish-brown when dried.

FRUIT SHAPE Elongated cone; apex pointed; truncate at peduncle attachment. Long wax type.

FLESH Thin walled.

PUNGENCY High; 7.

SUBSTITUTES Anaheim/New Mexican Chile, Costeño, Guajillo.

OTHER NAMES Chile Amarillo.

SOURCES FRESH: Not used fresh.

DRIED: Ethnic food stores and Mexican markets.

PREPARED: Not processed.

SEEDS: From the dried pods when you find them.

USES Cooked in incorporated sauces; for yellow color.

REMARKS This is another pepper which was being used by the Indians when Francisco Hernández came to America in 1570. Today it comes from the area around Oaxaca, Mexico. Any food cooked with it becomes a rich yellow color. I have never seen a fresh Chilcoztli; therefore I have not given the color.

Capsicum annuum var. *annuum*

Chilhuacle, dried

SIZE	2½ to 3 inches (6.4 to 7.6 cm) long; 1 to 2½ inches (2.5 to 6.4 cm) wide.
COLOR	Green to yellow, red, or black; dark when dried.
FRUIT SHAPE	Conical; lobate at peduncle attachment; apex pointed. Poblano type, but dries smooth.
FLESH	Medium thin walled.
PUNGENCY	Intermediate; 5.
SUBSTITUTES	Guajillo.
OTHER NAMES	Chilhuacle Amarillo, Chilhuacle Negro.
SOURCES	FRESH: Not used fresh. DRIED: Becoming more difficult to find. PREPARED: Not processed. SEEDS: Not available. Use from dried pods.
USES	For *moles*.
REMARKS	This pepper from the region around Oaxaca, Mexico, is expensive; perhaps this is the reason it is difficult to find. The name means "tomb chilli," probably in reference to its old, wrinkled appearance when dried; old chilli.

Capsicum annuum var. *glabriusculum*

Chiltepín (Chiltecpín) and **Chilpequín**, fresh and dried

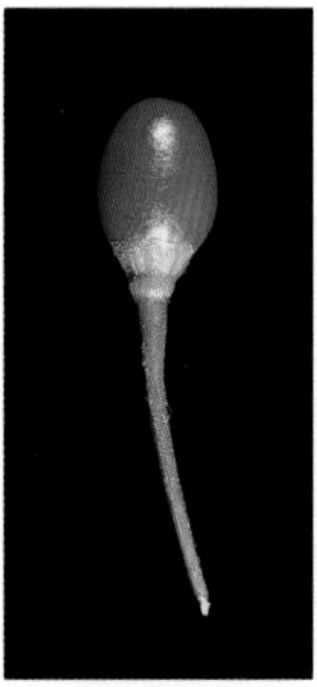

SIZE CHILTEPÍN: ¼ inch (.6 cm) long; ¾ inch (1.9 cm) wide.
CHILPEQUÍN: ½ to ¾ inch (1.3 to 1.9 cm) long; ¼ inch (.6 cm) wide.

COLOR FRESH: Green to red, some nearly black; glossy.
DRIED: Brownish red.

FRUIT SHAPE CHILTEPÍN: Ovoid; truncate at peduncle attachment.
CHILPEQUÍN: Conical; pointed apex.
Both with smooth cross sections.

FLESH Thin walled.

PUNGENCY Very high; 10+.

SUBSTITUTES Really nothing, but try Cayenne pepper, Thai peppers, Tabasco peppers (not the sauce).

OTHER NAMES Amash, Amomo, Bird, Bravo, Chililllo, Chilipiquín, Chilpaya, Chiltipiquín, Del Monte, Huarahuao, Max, Piquén, to name a few.

SOURCES FRESH: In the southernmost part of the Southwest, grows wild in backyards, fence rows, anywhere birds stop; in the rest of the country, found in some markets.
DRIED: Native Seeds/SEARCH, ethnic food markets, home gardens.
PREPARED: Some pickled in the Southwest; erratic availability in markets.
SEEDS: Native Seeds/SEARCH; specialty seed houses, friends in the Southwest. Ask your friendly neighborhood birds to help you.

USES Fresh or dried, mashed together with anything on your plate; table sauces; seasoning meats, vegetables, soups, and stews.

REMARKS Francisco Hernández, the first European to collect American plants systematically, described the tiny Chiltepín in 1615. Birds adore this pepper, but don't worry about birdburn. Our feathered friends lack the proper pain receptors for capsaicin. I once presented a paper to the Texas Pepper Conference titled "How to Make $10,000.00 per Acre." The largest audience which had attended the conference to date came to find out. I informed them an acre of Chiltepines was worth ten times an acre of Bell peppers—the problem was getting anyone to pick an acre of the tiny missiles. When I go to visit displaced Texans in other parts of the country I take a little package of Chiltepines, which I call "Texas Rubies" because of their value. The plant grows well in a pot if it is brought in during the winter—my eight-year-old plant now has a shrubby trunk. In nature, Chiltepines grow under nurse plants such as hackberry, where their seeds were dropped by fruit-eating birds.* The wild pepper seeds have passed through a bird's digestive system before germinating. Your seeds will need a good soak in warm water before planting in flats, plus patience.

President Thomas Jefferson grew Chiltepines from Texas seed acquired in 1813. Texas House Concurrent Resolution 82, introduced by Representative Bill Carter, made the Chiltepín the official native pepper of Texas in 1997.

*In 1997 Gary Paul Nabham, Ph.D., reported that "neither the wild nor the cultivated chili foliage fares as well in direct sunlight as it does in partial shade."

Capsicum annuum var. *annuum*

Costeño, dried

SIZE ¾ to 5½ inches (1.9 to 14 cm) long; ½ to 1¼ inches (1.3 to 3.2 cm) wide.

COLOR Light green to bright red. One type is yellow. Translucent when dry.

FRUIT SHAPE Highly variable. Conical to elongate; rugose; pointed apex; obtuse at the peduncle attachment; smooth cross section. Small red wax type.

FLESH Thin walled, translucent when dry.

PUNGENCY High; 8+.

SUBSTITUTES Cayenne, Chiltepín, Thai.

OTHER NAMES Chile Bandeño.

SOURCES FRESH: Only green, but not commonly used.
DRIED: Not commonly sold in USA. Occasionally in Mexican border markets. More regularly in regional Mexican markets, especially in Guerrero and Oaxaca.
PREPARED: Not processed.
SEEDS: From dried fruits.

USES Used in stews, soups, red sauces, *moles*, and to raise the pungency of sweeter, more flavorful varieties.

REMARKS This fruit can fool you because it is so very variable in shape and size. However, the transparency and broader shape separate it from similar types such as De Arbol, while the transparent Guajillo is larger and much darker in color. The yellow Costeño is quite expensive because less is grown. In August 1995 I was called upon to identify some peppers which were considered as evidence of some sort in a double murder case in west Texas. I determined the yellow Costeño from southern Mexico to be the pepper found at the scene of the crime. It was not, however, the murder weapon.

Cubanelle, fresh

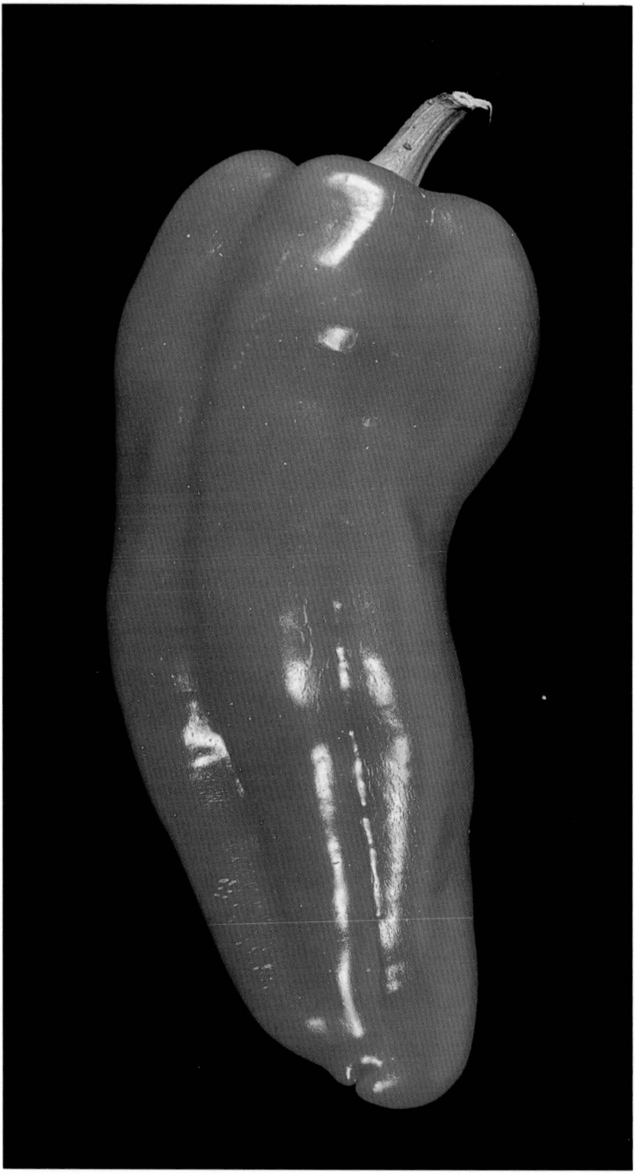

SIZE 6 inches (15.2 cm) long; 2¼ inches (5.7 cm) wide.

COLOR Pale yellow-green, to orange, to red; at times all those colors at once; glossy.

FRUIT SHAPE Elongated cylinder, undulating; sunken apex; lobate at peduncle attachment; corrugated cross section. Cuban or ethnic type.

FLESH Medium thick walled.

PUNGENCY Not pungent; 0.

SUBSTITUTES Red, yellow, or orange Bell pepper (green, if hard pressed); Banana; Szegedi; any sweet Cuban/ethnic type; Ají Flor.

OTHER NAMES Italian pepper.

SOURCES FRESH: Home gardens, farmer's markets, some ethnic food stores on the East Coast.
DRIED: Cannot be air-dried; perhaps can be dehydrated as you would Bell peppers.
PREPARED: Not processed.
SEEDS: Commercially available, but you may need to search the catalogs. Available cultivars: Biscayne, Cubanelle, Cubanelle PS.

USES Always used fresh: fried, in salads; as a vegetable, stuffed, in any recipe calling for a Bell pepper.

REMARKS Very flavorful! If you make enough demands, your grocer will carry them. I have seen them in markets in Philadelphia, where there is a large ethnic population.

Capsicum baccatum var. *pendulum*

Cusqueño, fresh and dried

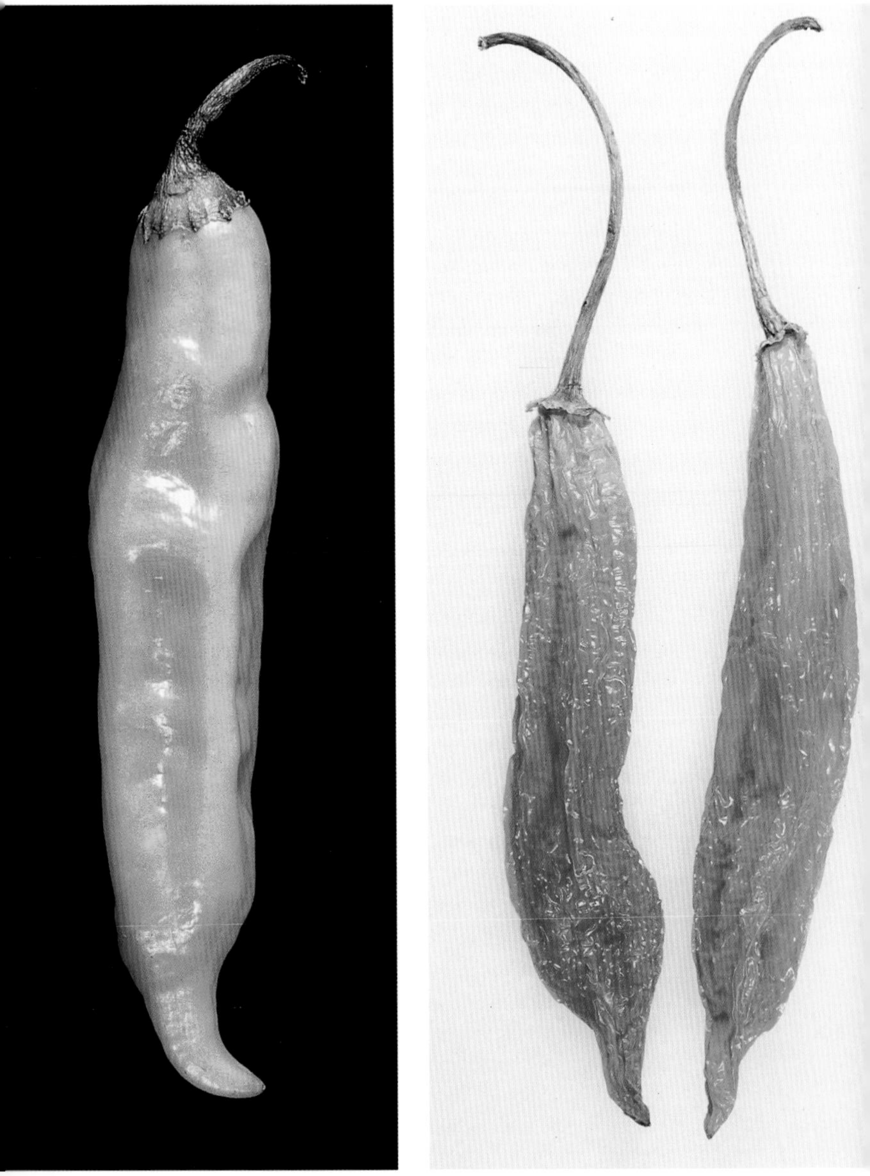

SIZE	4 to 6 inches (10.2 to 16.2 cm) long; ¾ to 1 inch (1.9 to 2.5 cm) wide at the peduncle attachment.
COLOR	Light green to golden yellow.
FRUIT SHAPE	Elongate; pointed apex; obtuse at peduncle attachment; intermediate corrugations. Andean Ají type.
FLESH	Thin walled.
PUNGENCY	High; 9 to 10.
SUBSTITUTES	Dried Habanero, dried Scotch Bonnet, dried Dátil.
OTHER NAMES	Andean Ají, Kellu-Uchu, Ají Verde, Ají Amarillo.
SOURCES	FRESH: Home gardens, specialty growers. See Ají Oro. DRIED: Not yet available commercially except from Sunset Farms. Dry your own. PREPARED: Not processed. SEEDS: Not readily available.
USES	In ceviche, table sauces, with potato dishes, stews.
REMARKS	A very common pepper in Peru, where it is primarily used in the dried form, but only becoming known in the United States since my book *Peppers: The Domesticated Capsicums*. Watch for it! In 1977 I brought the seed from Cuzco, Peru, where I found this large pepper to be the most common dried pepper in the market. It grew very well for me in both Corpus Christi and Austin, Texas, but never did attain the size of those in Peru. It is being grown at Sunset Farms.

Capsicum chinense

Dátil, fresh

SIZE 2 inches (5.1 cm) long; ¾ inch (1.9 cm) wide (midway).

COLOR Yellow-green to golden yellow.

FRUIT SHAPE Elongated with a slight neck; pointed apex; shallow wrinkles; obtuse at peduncle attachment; intermediate corrugation. Andean Ají type.

FLESH Thin walled.

PUNGENCY Very high to very, very high; 10.

SUBSTITUTES Habanero.

OTHER NAMES Mindoran, Minorcan.

SOURCES FRESH: Seasonally in home gardens, farmer's markets, food stores in and around St. Augustine, Florida.
DRIED: Heat-dried fruits available packaged in same area have little or no flavor.
PREPARED: Numerous sauces and relishes bottled in same area.
SEEDS: From growers in the St. Augustine, Florida, area.

USES In sauces, relishes, as a seasoning as one uses the Habanero. It is not recommended dried.

REMARKS Until the 1980s, the Dátil has been localized around St. Augustine, Florida since its introduction from the West Indies during the late colonial period two hundred years ago. I described Dátil in *Phytologia* 69 (1990): 413–415 and gave the historical background in the *Florida Historical Quarterly*, Fall 1995, pp. 132–147. Floridians use it green from a habit developed as a result of the poor keeping quality of *Capsicum chinense*, but it is much more pungent and flavorful in the golden, fully ripe stage. Let it ripen!

Capsicum annuum var. *annuum*

De Arbol, fresh and dried

SIZE 3 inches (7.6 cm) long; ⅜ inch (1 cm) wide.

COLOR FRESH: Green to red.
DRIED: Bright red.

FRUIT SHAPE Elongate conical, narrow at peduncle attachment; pointed apex; obtuse at peduncle attachment; slightly corrugated cross section. Cayenne type.

FLESH Thin walled.

PUNGENCY High; 7.

SUBSTITUTES FRESH: Serrano, green Thai, green Cayenne.
DRIED: Cayenne, Chiltepín, Japonés, dried Thai.

OTHER NAMES Alfilerillo, Bravo, Cola de Rata, Cuauhchilli, Ginnie pepper, Pico de Pájaro.

SOURCES FRESH: Seldom used fresh; home gardens in the United States.
DRIED: Found packaged or in bulk in the spice section of many supermarkets and ethnic food stores.
PREPARED: Not processed.
SEEDS: Catalogs of specialty seed companies; from packaged dried fruits.

USES In table sauces, soups, stews, cooked sauces, and to pep up milder peppers.

REMARKS De Arbol, tree chile, is a very common Mexican pepper which is one of the few with the same name whether fresh or dried. Put a couple in your bottle of vinegar or tequila.

Capsicum annuum var. *annuum*

Guajillo, dried

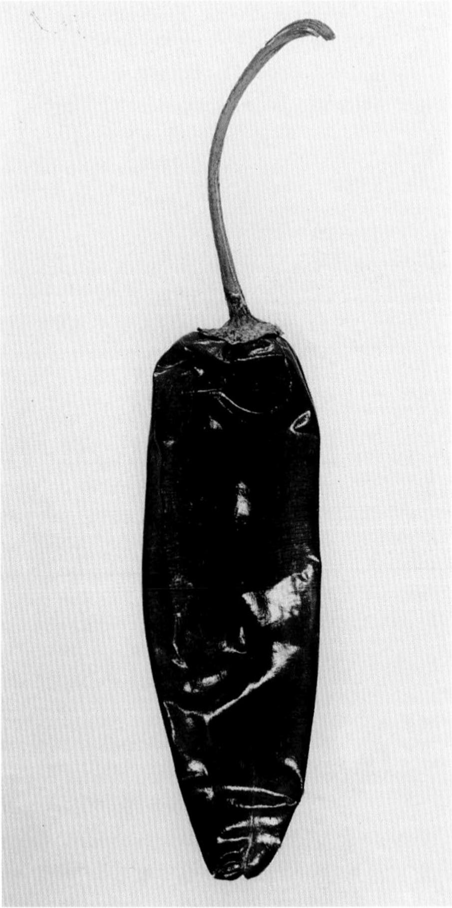

SIZE	3 to 5 inches (7.6 to 12.7) long; ½ to 1¼ inches (1.3 to 3.2 cm) wide, very variable.
COLOR	FRESH: Green to red to brownish red. DRIED: Translucent reddish brown.
FRUIT SHAPE	Elongate conical; pointed apex; obtuse at peduncle attachment; smooth cross section. Cayenne type.
FLESH	Thin walled, translucent when dried.
PUNGENCY	Intermediate; 5.
SUBSTITUTES	Dried Cascabel, Anaheim/New Mexican Chile.
OTHER NAMES	FRESH: Mirasol, Puya. DRIED: Cascabel, Pulla, Pullia, Puya (preferred spelling), Travieso, Trompa; perhaps Costeño and Chilhuacle.
SOURCES	FRESH: See Mirasol. DRIED: Primarily in the Southwest or in ethnic food stores. PREPARED: Not processed. SEEDS: Catalogs of specialty seed catalogs. Available cultivars: La Blanca 74, Loreto 74, Real Mirasol.
USES	Sauces, seasoning, color in cookery, color extraction.
REMARKS	Because the Guajillo seeds rattle in the dried pod, it is often mislabeled Cascabel, the round pepper which also rattles. High coloring quality! The dried Anaheim/New Mexican Chile is often packaged and mislabeled as Guajillo. Look at the picture above and check the pods in the package. Neither Anaheim/New Mexican Chile nor Cascabel has the flavor or coloring power of the Guajillo. When fresh green, it is called Mirasol (see pages 120–121).

Capsicum chinense

Habanero, fresh and freeze-dried

SIZE 1 to 2½ inches (2.5 to 6.4 cm) long; 1 inch (2.5 cm) wide.

COLOR Green to yellow-orange, or orange, or orange-red.

FRUIT SHAPE Campanulate, undulating; pointed apex; truncate at peduncle attachment; cross section with intermediate corrugations. Habanero type.

FLESH Thin walled.

PUNGENCY Very, very high; 10+.

SUBSTITUTES Nothing can match its flavor and aroma, but try five Jalapeños for each Habanero, or one Dátil, one Scotch Bonnet, or one and one-half Rocoto.

OTHER NAMES Congo, Bonda Man Jacques, Bonnie, Ginnie pepper, Guinea pepper, Pimenta do Chiero, Siete Caldos, Scotch Bonnet, and Pimienta do Cheiro in Brazil.

SOURCES FRESH: Some markets on the East Coast catering to Caribbean people, home gardens; increasingly in supermarkets and specialty food stores.

DRIED: Will not dry well on the bush. The dehydrated ones being sold have only heat; the flavor which distinguishes the fresh Habanero is all gone.

PREPARED: Bottled sauces, canned; in specialty shops and some supermarkets.

SEEDS: Catalogs of some specialty seed companies; becoming easier to find. Available cultivars: Habanero, Red Savina at Shepherd's.

USES In table sauces, cooked sauces, as a seasoning; essential oil extraction.

REMARKS The true Habanero is golden orange or orange-red, never red. However, among *C. chinense* are some red Habanero types such as West Indian Red, and others used for bottled sauces in Costa Rica and other tropical locations where *C. chinense* grows. The SUPER pungent Red Savina developed from a sport and sold by Shepherd's Garden Seeds is five times more pungent than the golden Habanero. It is probably best used as a source of capsaicin for medicinal purposes. The dried Habanero is not a pepper I would recommend using until a process of drying to retain flavor and aroma is developed. I attended a pepper convention where Habaneros were served dipped in chocolate like strawberries. "Not funny, McGee." Unless you are a masochist, don't do it.

Capsicum annuum var. *annuum*

Jalapeño, fresh and smoke dried

SIZE 3 inches (7.6 cm) long; 1½ inches (3.8 cm) wide.

COLOR Bright to deep blackish green; matures red.

FRUIT SHAPE Elongate cylindrical; blunt apex; obtuse at peduncle attachment; smooth cross section. Jalapeño type.

FLESH Medium thick walled.

PUNGENCY Low to high, according to season, soil conditions, state of maturity, and cultivar (see Remarks); 4 to 8.

SUBSTITUTES Caloro, Caribe, Fresno, Santa Fe Grande, Serrano.

OTHER NAMES Acorchado, Bola, Bolita, Candelaria, Cuaresmeño, Gorda, Huachinango, Jarocho, Mora, Morita.

SOURCES FRESH: Most supermarkets (it is becoming more readily available throughout the United States); although some Jalapeños are raised by commercial growers in the Southwest, most are imported from Mexico; home gardens.

DRIED: Will not air dry, must be smoked. Smoked peppers are called *chipotles*, and when *chipotles* are canned with vinegar, they are *adobado*.

PREPARED: Canned sliced or whole, pickled (*en escabeche*), prepared with other canned and frozen foods; in cheeses, sauces/salsas, candies, etc.

SEEDS: Most seed suppliers will have at least one cultivar. Available cultivars: Early Jalapeño, Espinalteco, Jalapa, Jalapeño M, Jaloro (yellow), Jarocho, Jumbo Jal, Mitla, Papaloapan, Peludo, Pinalteco, Rayado, San Andrés, 76104, TAM Mild Jalapeño-1 (also -2), TAM Sweet Jalapeño, TAM Veracruz.

USES In condiments, sauces/salsas, soups, stews, meat and vegetable dishes, appetizers, desserts, as garnishes, for processing. A sought-after variety, the Meco, with striations/corking in horizontal lines on the fruit, originated near Chiapas, Mexico. Mora, a fatter variety with striations/corking lengthwise or vertical on the fruit, comes from Hildalgo, Mexico. The Mora is a much smaller Jalapeño *chipotle*, while the Morita is a dried, unsmoked Serrano.

REMARKS The Jalapeño originated near Jalapa, Mexico. It crossed the Texas-Mexico border after World War II. The thick-walled fruit does not dry well; therefore it is smoked by a pre-Columbian method. Any fully ripe pepper can be smoked. When smoked, chilli peppers become *chipotles* (*chilpotle*), which is a modern corruption of the Nahuatl word for smoked chilli—*pochchilli* (*pochilli*). Jalapeños are the peppers most commonly smoked commercially. Canned smoked peppers are packed in vinegar and labeled *adobado* (pickled). Dr. Ben Villalon at Texas A&M University has bred TAM Mild and another which is not pungent at all, which he designed to be canned with controlled amounts of capsaicin added and labeled accordingly. Pace Foods, a division of Campbell Soup Company, has developed a big, 4-to-7-inch, no-heat Jalapeño to make an "extra mild" Jalapeño salsa. Whatever happened to Jalapeño roulette?

Although it is undeserving because it is such a recent immigrant compared to the Chiltepín, a fun-loving Texas legislature declared the Jalapeño to be the state pepper of Texas in 1995.

Capsicum annuum var. *annuum*

Japonés, fresh and dried

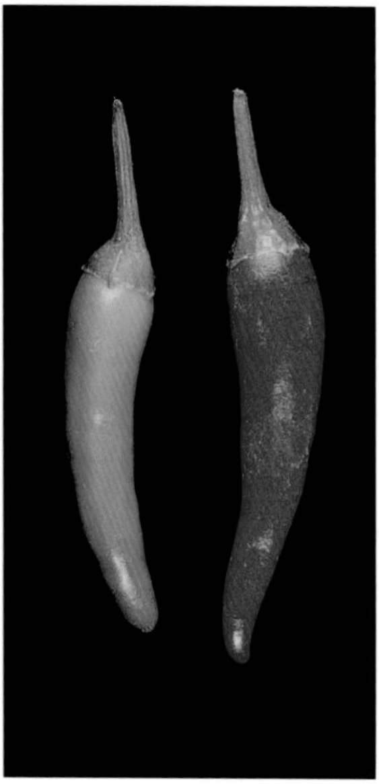

SIZE 2 inches (5.1 cm) long; ½ inch (1.3 cm) wide.
COLOR Green to red.
FRUIT SHAPE Elongate; pointed apex; obtuse at peduncle; smooth cross section. Small Cayenne type.
FLESH Thin walled.
PUNGENCY High; 7.
SUBSTITUTES De Arbol, Thai, Cayenne.
OTHER NAMES None known.
SOURCES FRESH: Not sold fresh.
DRIED: Most food stores have it packaged in the spice section.
PREPARED: Not processed.
SEEDS: Get them from the dried, packaged fruits.
USES To pep up milder peppers; in stews, soups, cooked sauces, curries, Thai dishes.
REMARKS No one seems to know with certainty, but the Japonés is probably of Japanese origin, hence the name. It has been called a dried Serrano, but after growing seed from packaged Japonés I can vouch it is not a Serrano. Hontaka and Santaka, peppers of Japanese origin, are very similar to the Japonés.

Mirasol, fresh

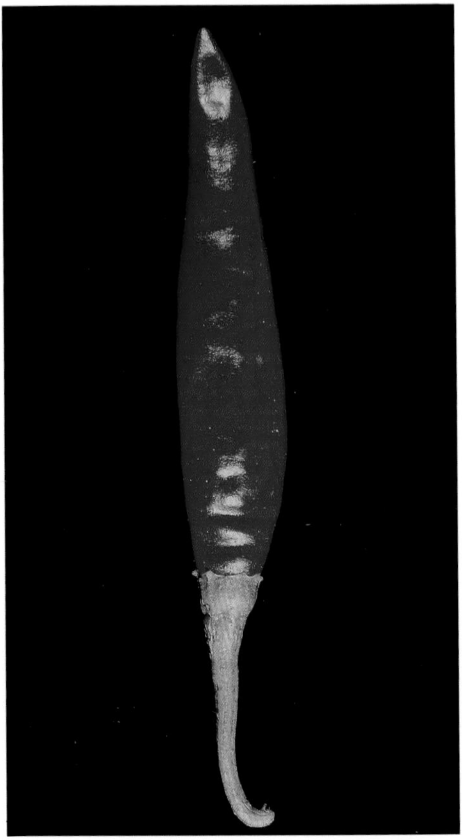

SIZE 3 to 5 inches (7.6 to 12.7 cm) long; ½ to 1¼ inches (1.3 to 3.2 cm) wide, very variable.

COLOR Green to red to brownish red.

FRUIT SHAPE Elongate conical; pointed apex; obtuse at peduncle attachment; smooth cross section. Cayenne type.

FLESH Thin walled.

PUNGENCY Intermediate; 5.

SUBSTITUTES Serrano, Jalapeño, Thai.

OTHER NAMES Many peppers are called *mirasol* ("look at the sun") because the pepper is erect and appears to be pointing toward the sun in its early stages. Guajillo.

SOURCES FRESH: Not yet available in markets in the United States; home gardens.
DRIED: See Guajillo.
PREPARED: Not processed.
SEEDS: Catalogs of specialty seed suppliers. Available cultivars: La Blanca 74, Loreto 74, Real Mirasol.

USES In table sauces; used like the Serrano.

REMARKS The fruit is usually erect in the juvenile stage, but as it gets larger and ripens, it tends to droop from its own weight so that it is no longer looking at the sun. Mirasol is the name for the fresh state of the Guajillo (see pages 108–109).

Capsicum annuum var. *annuum*

Mulato, dried

SIZE 4 inches (10.2 cm) long; 2½ inches (6.4 cm) wide.

COLOR Dark brown.

FRUIT SHAPE Flattened, wrinkled; lobate at peduncle attachment; intermediate corrugations. Poblano type.

FLESH Medium thick walled.

PUNGENCY Low to intermediate; 3 to 5.

SUBSTITUTES Ancho, Pasilla.

OTHER NAMES Ancho, Pasilla.

SOURCES FRESH: See Poblano.

DRIED: Imported from Mexico, sold in food stores throughout the Southwest, usually in mixed lots with Ancho.

PREPARED: Canned *mole* sauce now available where Mexican products are sold.

SEEDS: A few specialty seed suppliers carry it, but the Poblano/Mulato does not produce typical fruit when grown in the United States except in the Oxnard, California area. Available cultivars: Mulato V-2, Roque.

USES In sauces such as *mole poblano* used on turkey and chicken. Has a deep, rich flavor which is compatible with chocolate.

REMARKS The name refers to its dark color. The fresh Mulato is brown or *achocolatado* (chocolate colored) when mature. After the dried Mulato has been soaked it will remain brown. Use some ground Mulato in your chocolate dishes to enhance the flavor of the chocolate. The Mulato is the dried state of the varieties of Poblano which are brown at maturity (see pages 132–134).

Capsicum annuum var. *annuum*

Pasilla, dried

SIZE 6 to 12 inches (15.2 to 30.5 cm) long; ¾ to 1¾ inches (1.9 to 4.5 cm) wide.

COLOR Dried, dark blackish brown, raisin colored.

FRUIT SHAPE Elongate, flattened, irregular, wrinkled; pointed apex; obtuse at peduncle attachment; corrugated cross section. Anaheim/New Mexican Chile type.

FLESH Medium thick walled.

PUNGENCY Low to intermediate; 3 to 5.

SUBSTITUTES FRESH: Poblano. DRIED: Mulato, Ancho.

OTHER NAMES Ancho, Apaseo, Pabellón.

SOURCES FRESH: Probably not sold commercially outside Mexico; home gardens.

DRIED: Many supermarkets in the Southwest; some ethnic food stores.

PREPARED: Made into paste which is formed in small squares and dried. This is called *pasado*.

SEEDS: Catalogs of specialty seed houses. Available cultivars: Apaseo and Pabellón 1.

USES In table sauces; as a garnish and condiment in soups; essential to *mole* and other cooked sauces.

REMARKS This Mexican pepper has a rich, mellow flavor which complements chocolate. *Pasilla* means raisin and refers to the color. This narrow pepper is mistakenly called Ancho in northwestern Mexico and southern California. California recipes calling for the Pasilla may mean Poblano/Ancho. The Pasilla is too narrow to be stuffed (*relleno*). This misnomer causes much confusion. I asked the manager of the huge Tianguis Latin American food store in Los Angeles why he reversed the names of Pasilla and Ancho. He replied, "We use the name given to us by the grower." To add to the confusion, there is a Pasilla de Oaxaca which looks more like a brown Guajillo/Mirasol. The Oaxaca Pasilla is probably the progenitor of the Anaheim/New Mexican Chile.

Capsicum annuum var. *annuum*

Pepperoncini, fresh

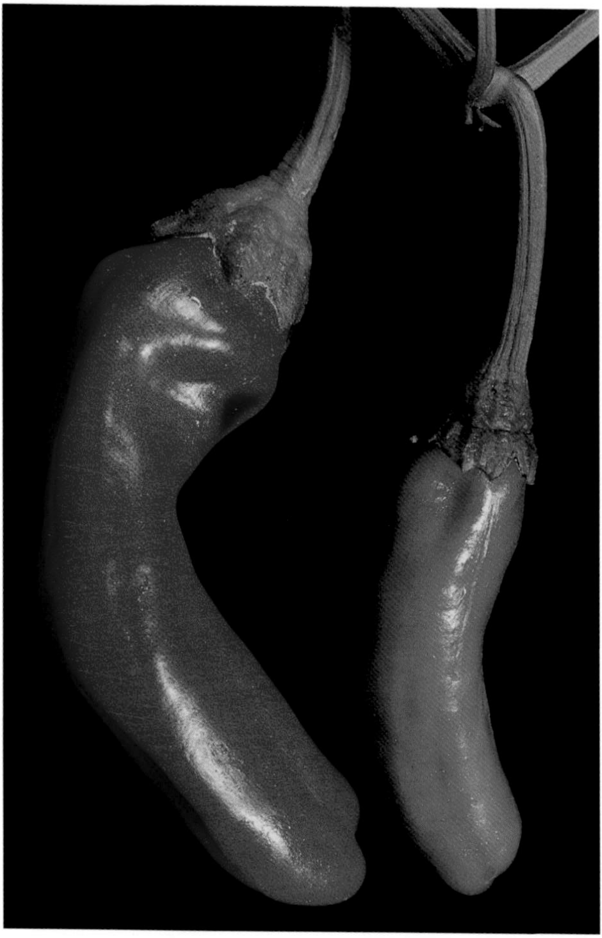

SIZE 3 to 5 inches (7.6 to 12.7 cm) long; ¾ inches (1.9 cm) wide at the peduncle attachment.

COLOR Green to red; at least one golden cultivar.

FRUIT SHAPE Elongated cylinder, pointed apex, wrinkled; slightly truncate at peduncle attachment; corrugated cross section. Cuban/Ethnic type.

FLESH Medium thick walled.

PUNGENCY Not pungent to low; 0 to 1.

SUBSTITUTES Golden Greek, Pepperone.

OTHER NAMES None.

SOURCES FRESH: Home gardens, farmer's markets.
DRIED: Not dried.
PREPARED: Pickled, in most food stores.
SEEDS: Most large seed company catalogs, specialty seed suppliers. Available cultivars: Golden Greek, Pepperoncini.

USES Green fruit pickled with salads; pickling.

REMARKS Introduced from Italy, where no salad maker would be caught dead without a Pepperoncini.

Capsicum annuum var. *annuum*

Peter Pepper, fresh

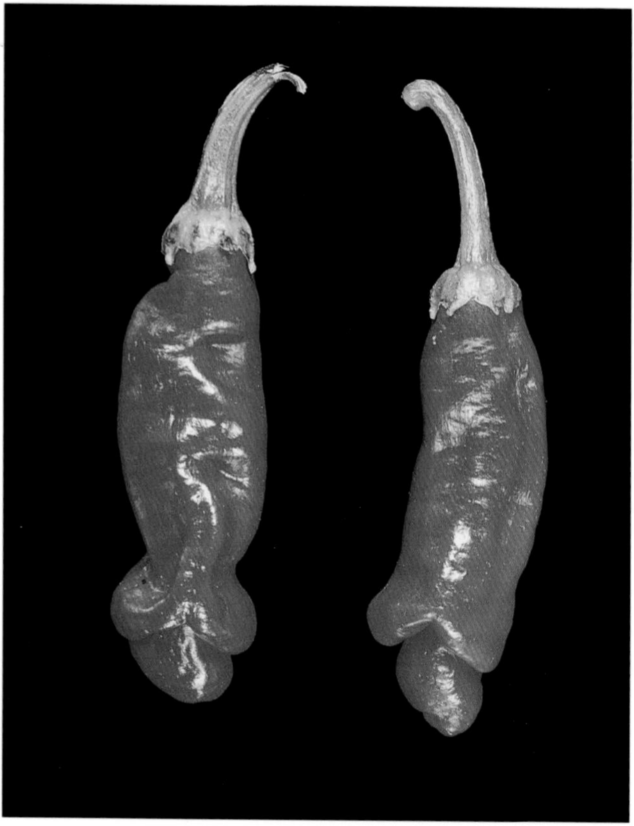

SIZE 3 inches (7.6 cm) long; ½ to ¾ inches (1.3 to 1.9 cm) wide at the peduncle attachment.

COLOR Green to red; at least one golden cultivar.

FRUIT SHAPE Elongated cylinder; obtuse at peduncle attachment; cross section with intermediate corrugations; apex highly variable and suggestive. Small hot type.

FLESH Medium thick walled.

PUNGENCY Intermediate to high; 5 to 8.

SUBSTITUTES Some of the *Capsicum baccatum* var. *pendulum* have the same form in the juvenile stage but grow out of it as they mature.

OTHER NAMES Penis pepper.

SOURCES FRESH: Home gardens, farmer's markets.
DRIED: It will dry well.
PREPARED: Not commercially prepared.
SEEDS: Some specialty seed company catalogs.

USES In table sauces, but mainly as decoration or as a conversation piece.

REMARKS Even ornamental peppers are edible, but there is a limit to what I'd bite into. It is amusing to use this pepper in your bottles of herb vinegar or tequila. See page 54 for an explanation of the peculiar shape of this pepper.

Capsicum annuum var. *annuum*

Pimento / Pimiento, fresh

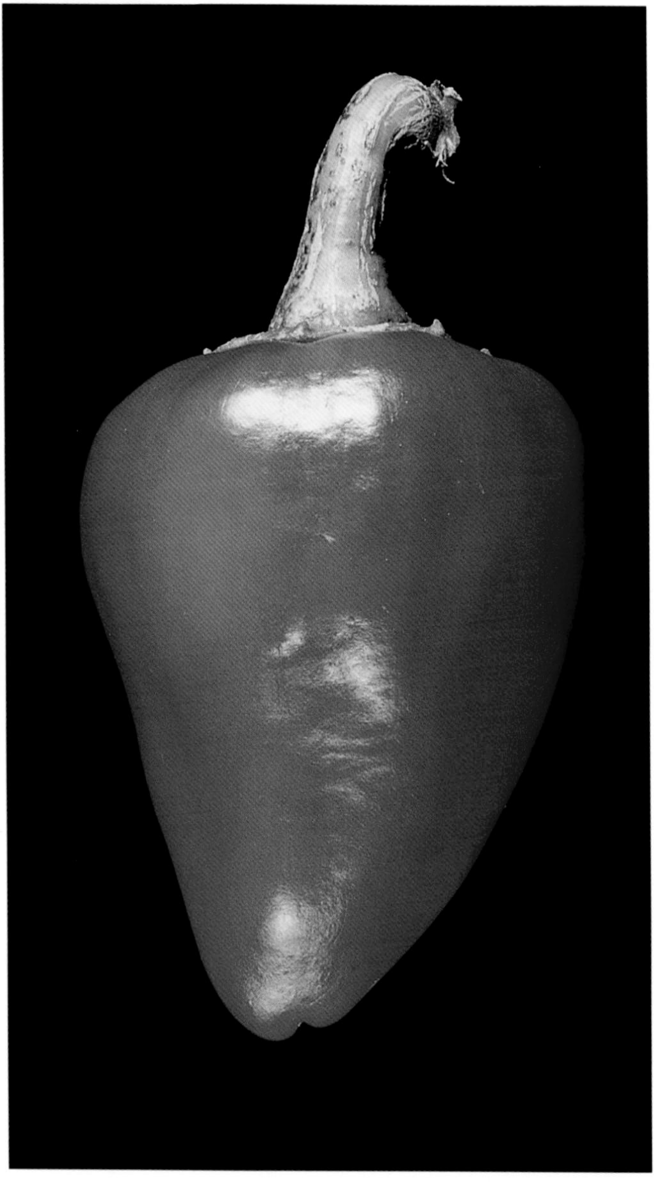

SIZE 4½ inches (11.4 cm) long; 3½ inches (8.9 cm) wide at the peduncle attachment.

COLOR Usually green to red, but some cultivars are yellow or orange; glossy.

FRUIT SHAPE Conical, pointed apex, often heart-shape; truncate at peduncle attachment; smooth cross section. Some may be tomato-shaped. Pimento type.

FLESH Thick walled.

PUNGENCY Not pungent; 0.

SUBSTITUTES Red Bell pepper, Tomato pepper, Cheese pepper.

OTHER NAMES Pimiento.

SOURCES FRESH: Home gardens, farmer's markets, occasionally in food markets.

DRIED: Dehydrated.

PREPARED: Canned, common in supermarkets.

SEEDS: Catalogs of most large seed companies. Available cultivars: Bighart, Canada Cheese, Mississippi Nemaheart, Perfection, Pimiento Select, Pimiento-L, Sunnybrook, Truhart Perfection, Truhart, Perfection-D, Yellow Cheese.

USES FRESH: in salads or in any recipe calling for Bell pepper.

CANNED: in casseroles, cheese spreads, garnishes, to stuff olives; for color extraction.

REMARKS The Pimento type fruits were introduced from Spain. The canned Pimento industry, which followed the 1914 invention of a roasting machine to facilitate peeling, is almost a thing of the past due to the regular appearance of the red Bell pepper in the markets. Grow the Pimento yourself because it is so much more flavorful in salads and other dishes in place of the Bell pepper.

Capsicum annuum var. *annuum*

Poblano, fresh

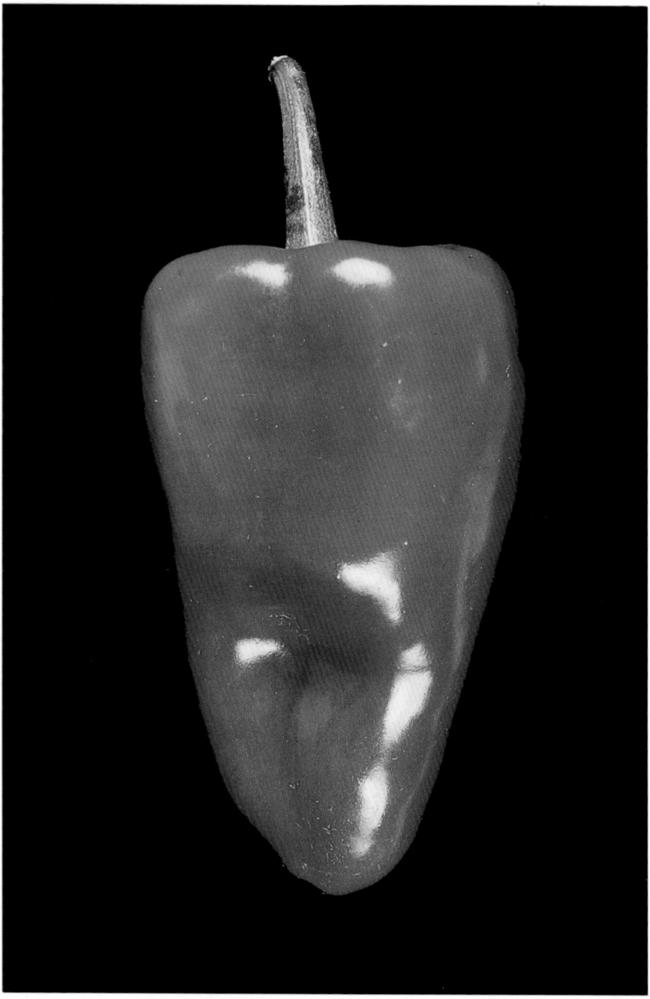

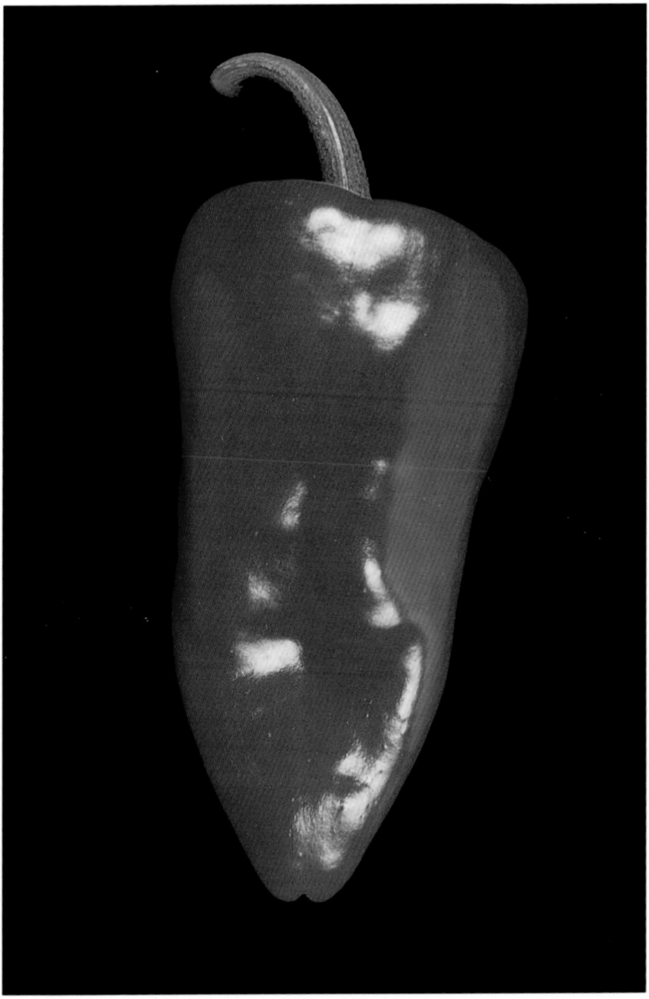

SIZE 4 inches (10.2 cm) long; 2½ inches (6.4 cm) wide.

COLOR Dark green; matures red (Ancho) or brown (Mulato). See pages 68–69 and 122–123.

FRUIT SHAPE Conical; tapered to a blunt point at apex; wrinkled; lobate at peduncle attachment; intermediate corrugations. Poblano type.

FLESH Medium thick walled.

PUNGENCY Low to high; 3 to 7.

SUBSTITUTES Mexi-Bell, Anaheim / New Mexican Chile.

OTHER NAMES Ancho, Chile para Rellenar, Joto, Mexican Chile, Mulato, Pasilla.

SOURCES FRESH: Food stores throughout the Southwest. More food stores in other parts of the country are carrying it in the imported produce section.

DRIED: See Ancho and Mulato.

PREPARED: Not processed.

SEEDS: Specialty seed suppliers. Poblano does not always produce typical fruit in the United States, except in the area around Oxnard, California. Available cultivars: Ancho, Ancho Esmeralda, Chorro, Miahuateco, Mulato Roque, Verdeño.

USES Stuffed or *relleno*, strips or *rajas*, in soups and sauces. Roast, seed, and peel before using; dehydration.

REMARKS This pre-Columbian pepper is the most used pepper in Mexico. The green stages of the Ancho and the Mulato look just alike and are called Poblano. Mexican peppers nearly all have different names for the dried and the fresh stages. Poblano means from Pueblo, Mexico, the center of its growth. In California the Poblano is often miscalled Pasilla.

Rocotillo, fresh

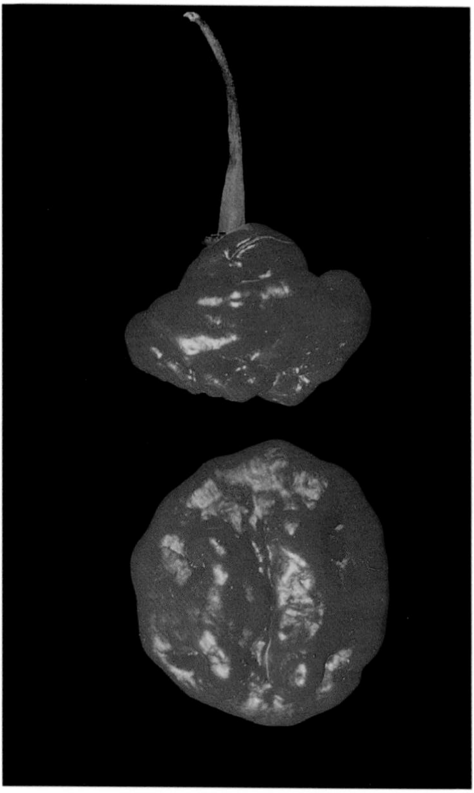

SIZE 1½ to 2 inches (3.8 to 5.1 cm) long; 1½ to 2 inches (3.8 to 5.1 cm) wide.

COLOR Green to deep red.

FRUIT SHAPE Campanulate; slightly lobate at peduncle attachment; cross section with intermediate corrugations. Scotch Bonnet type.

FLESH Medium thick walled.

PUNGENCY Low; 1 to 3.

SUBSTITUTES For garnish use Squash pepper; in dishes use red Bell peppers with a dash of Cayenne pepper.

OTHER NAMES Pimiento. Rocotillo (little Rocoto) is the name given to me when I first got the pepper in Peru.

SOURCES FRESH: Home gardens.
DRIED: Not used dried.
PREPARED: Not yet processed.
SEEDS: Difficult to find. Many sell similar-shaped *Capsicum annuum* var. *annuum* for this pepper. True Rocotillo grows in clusters of two to five pendant fruits at a node.

USES Beautiful as a garnish, whole for snacks, in salads, or as you would use a red Bell pepper.

REMARKS When I introduced the Rocotillo to the USA in 1984, I said it was my "hands down favorite eating pepper." Since then the Ají Flor from Brazil runs a close second. I lost the Rocotillo seed from the original depicted in *Peppers: The Domesticated Capsicums* but still yearn for them. A few growers, nevertheless, have perpetuated my original seed in Corpus Christi and Edinburg, Texas. From things which have happened trying to locate seed for this pepper in Peru since 1990, I have about concluded the name Rocotillo may be given to all *Capsicum chinense* in Peru, but I have not been able to confirm this.

Rocoto, fresh

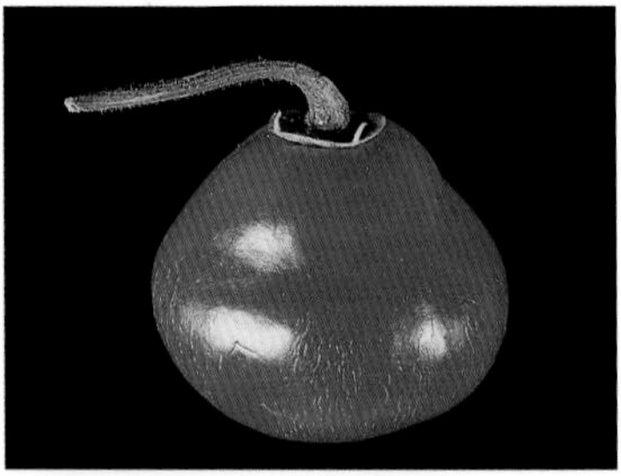

SIZE 1 to 1½ inches (2.5 to 3.8 cm) long; 1 to 1½ inches (2.5 to 3.8 cm) wide.

COLOR Green to golden yellow or red.

FRUIT SHAPE Globose to oblate; truncate at peduncle attachment; smooth cross section. Some have definite necks. Its own type.

FLESH Medium thick walled.

PUNGENCY Seems very, very, very high but actually has a Scoville lower than Habanero (see Remarks below); 9 to 10.

SUBSTITUTES Nothing really, but try one-half to one Habanero or two or three Jalapeños for one Rocoto.

OTHER NAMES Caballo (Guatemala and bordering Chiapas, Mexico), Canario, Manzana, and Perón in Mexico; in Costa Rica it is Manzana but more often Jalapeño.

SOURCES FRESH: Latin American food markets.
DRIED: Not dried.
PREPARED: Not available.
SEEDS: Perhaps a specialty seed catalog.

USES In table sauces, as a seasoning, stuffed, in vegetable and meat dishes.

REMARKS The black seeds make this pungent pepper easy to identify. I had Scoville heat tests run on the Rocoto several times because I could not believe it rated lower than Habanero—they must have made a mistake because I can't eat it. In the tests the capsaicin is lower than the capsaicin of the Habanero; however, the dihydrocapsaicin and nordihydrocapsaicin are higher. Both of these capsaicinoids affect different parts of the mouth than CAPS; perhaps this accounts for its extreme effect—*quién sabe*? These may not have more CAPS than other highly pungent peppers, but they may cause delayed pain in more sensitive locations than those affected by capsaicin alone.

Romanian, fresh

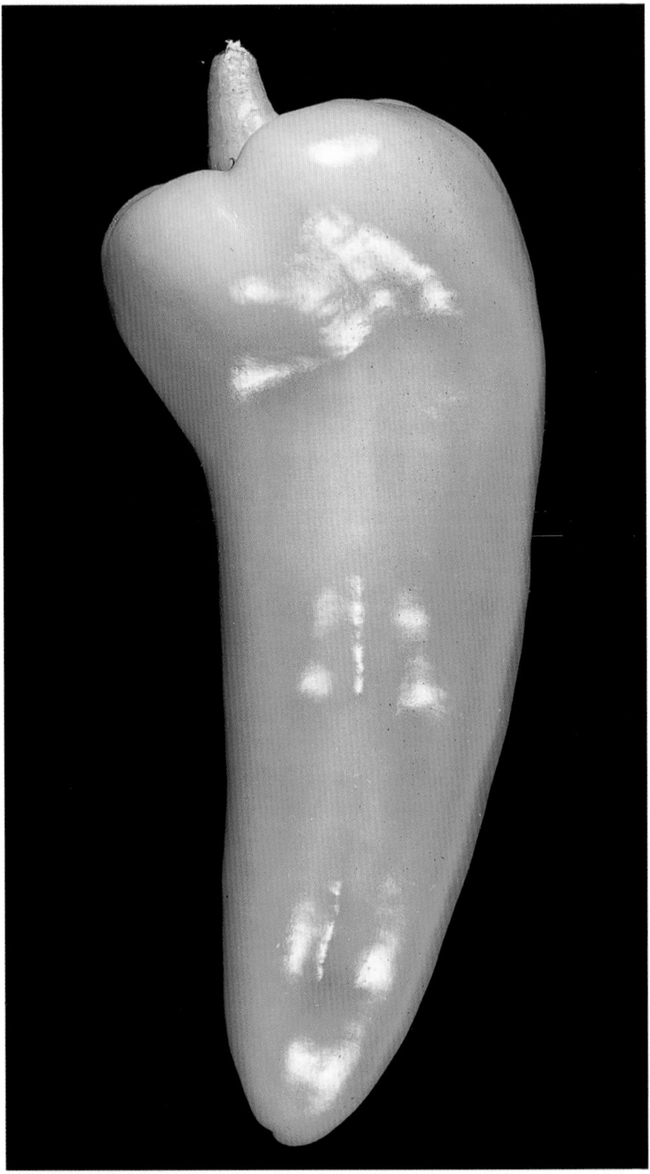

SIZE 6½ inches (16.5 cm) long; 1½ inches (3.8 cm) wide.

COLOR Yellow-green to deep orange.

FRUIT SHAPE Elongate with a sunken apex; lobate at the peduncle attachment; cross section with intermediate corrugation. Cuban/Ethnic type.

FLESH Thick walled.

PUNGENCY Not pungent.

SUBSTITUTES Colored Bells, Cubanelle, any sweet ethnic type such as Kolaska, Gypsy, Italian Sweet, Szegedi, etc.

OTHER NAMES Similar ethnic peppers such as Cubanelle.

SOURCES FRESH: Home gardens, ethnic food stores, farmer's markets.
DRIED: Not dried.
PREPARED: Not processed.
SEEDS: Major seed catalogs.

USES In salads, stews, and as the Cubanelle; great for frying.

REMARKS A very tasty pepper which would be used more if available. There are a number of look-alikes with similar flavor which are great for frying or for roasting and peeling and then putting in a covered container with olive oil, garlic, a little vinegar, and basil to be refrigerated and used in salads and on sandwiches.

Capsicum annuum var. *annuum*

Romesco, fresh and dried

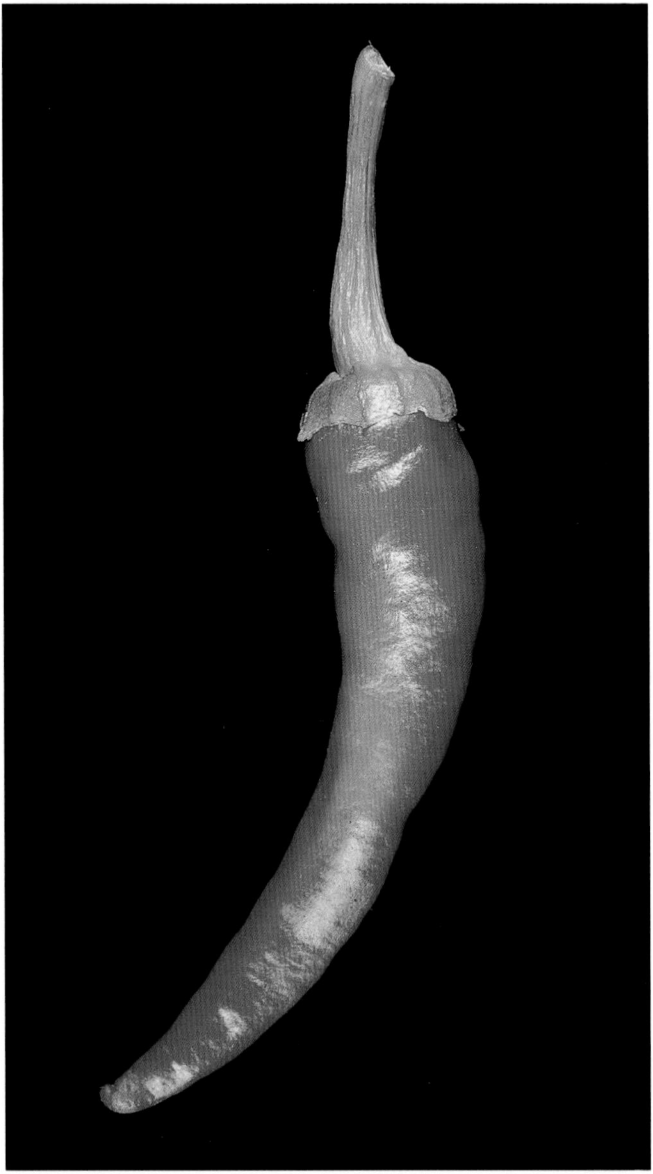

SIZE 5 to 6 inches (12.7 to 15.2 cm) long; ½ to ¾ inches (1.3 to 1.9 cm) wide.

COLOR Green to red.

FRUIT SHAPE Elongate, tapering to a point, curved; obtuse at peduncle attachment; slightly corrugated cross section. Cayenne type.

FLESH Medium thick walled.

PUNGENCY Intermediate to high; 5 to 7.

SUBSTITUTES Dried or fresh Cayenne, Thai, Turkish depending on recipe.

OTHER NAMES Not known.

SOURCES FRESH: Home gardens.
DRIED: Ethnic food market, maybe?
PREPARED: Powdered, ground, but not commercially in the USA.
SEEDS: From your friends who travel to Spain.

USES In sauces such as the traditional Romesco Sauce of Spain, which contains bread and is eaten with seafood (see *Red Hot Peppers*, page 152).

REMARKS This pepper and its seed were sent to me from Spain by Elizabeth Lambert Ortiz, an expert on Latin American and Spanish cookery. It seems to be a little more robust in flavor and less pungent than the Cajun/ Louisiana Cayenne.

Santa Fe Grande, fresh

Courtesy Petoseed

SIZE 3 inches (7.6 cm) long; 1½ inches (3.8 cm) wide at the peduncle attachment.

COLOR Pale greenish yellow to orange to red; glossy.

FRUIT SHAPE Conical, pointed apex; truncate at peduncle attachment; smooth cross section. Long wax type.

FLESH Thick walled.

PUNGENCY Intermediate to high; 5 to 7.

SUBSTITUTES Any pungent yellow pepper, Cascabella, Floral Gem, Hungarian Wax.

OTHER NAMES Caloro, Caribe, Cera, Güero.

SOURCES FRESH: Many food markets, home gardens, farmer's markets.
DRIED: Dehydration.
PREPARED: Pickled, infrequently found in food stores.
SEEDS: Catalogs of specialty seed houses; some of the larger seed companies' catalogs. Available cultivars: Caloro PS, Caloro, Caribe, Grande Gold (sweet), Hybrid Gold Spike, Santa Fe Grande, TAM Rio.

USES Table sauces, pickled, seasoning, processing.

REMARKS Most Santa Fe Grandes found in American markets are grown in Mexico, where because of their "bite" they are called Caribe, after the allegedly cannibalistic Carib Indians who inhabited the West Indies when Columbus first arrived--they are one and the same pepper. The Caloro, which was developed by crossing Fresno and Floral Gem, is also virtually the same pepper. Santa Fe Grande/Caribe and Caloro are used in the immature yellow stage when they are known as *güeros* (blonds). Each matures to red and can be used when fully ripe; however, it will be more pungent than the yellow ones. For some reason, few commercial growers plant Fresno and Floral Gem today.

Capsicum chinense

Scotch Bonnet, fresh

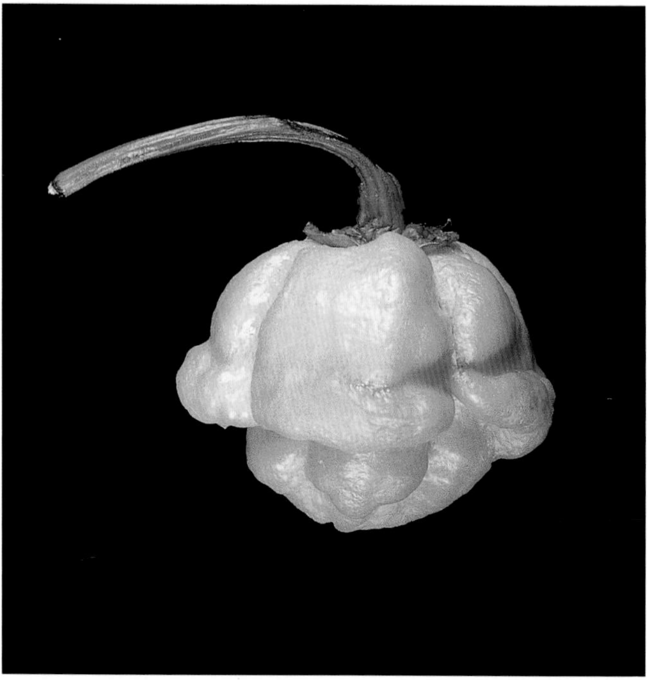

SIZE 2 to 2½ inches (5.1 to 6.4 cm) in diameter; 1¼ to 1½ inches (3.2 to 3.8 cm) deep.

COLOR Green to yellow-orange or orange.

FRUIT SHAPE Campanulate; apex sunken; lobate at peduncle attachment; very corrugated cross section. Scotch Bonnet type.

FLESH Thin walled.

PUNGENCY Very, very high; 10+.

SUBSTITUTES Habanero, Dátil, West Indian Hot, several Serranos.

OTHER NAMES Scot's Bonnet, Bonnie.

SOURCES FRESH: Markets catering to West Indians, home gardens.

DRIED: Does not dry well; retains pungency but loses flavor.

PREPARED: Bottled sauces in specialty shops.

SEEDS: Catalogs of some specialty seed companies; not easily found.

USES In table sauces, cooked sauces, as seasoning.

REMARKS The name refers to its shape like the Scot's Tam o'Shanter, a cap with a tight headband and a full flat top with a large pompom, or like a small flying saucer. The deeply inverted, always rounded apex folds into a crimped periphery. In the past Scotch Bonnet has been confused with Habanero. The most typical Scotch Bonnets are grown in Jamaica. Many globular, golden *Capsicum chinense* grown in the Caribbean islands are called Scotch Bonnet, and most taste about the same even though they do not have the typical bonnet shape, which is rounded, not pointed, at the apex. Growers in most of those islands make no effort to keep their *C. chinense* from crossing, hence the confusing plethora of shapes. If you save the seed, you might get almost anything—red, yellow, orange; round, elongate, campanulate.

Serrano, fresh

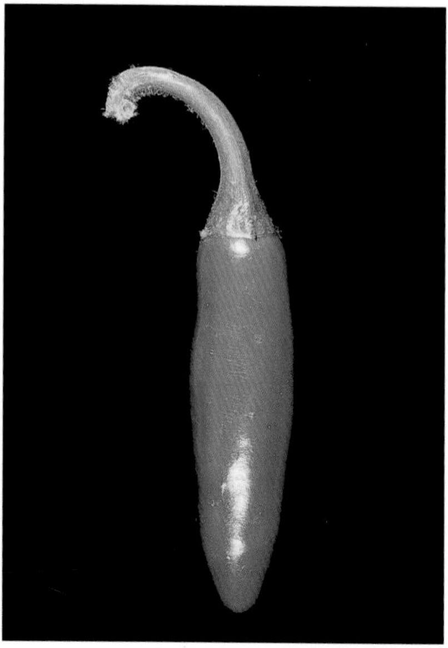

SIZE 2¼ inches (5.7 cm) long; ½ inch (1.3 cm) wide.

COLOR Green to red, glossy.

FRUIT SHAPE Elongated cylinder; blunt apex; obtuse at peduncle attachment; smooth cross section. Serrano type.

FLESH Thick walled.

PUNGENCY Intermediate to high; 6 to 8.

SUBSTITUTES Chiltepín, Fresno, Jalapeño, Thai.

OTHER NAMES Balín, Chile Verde, Cora, Morita, Serranito, Típico.

SOURCES FRESH: Most food markets, but less common than the Jalapeño; home gardens, farmer's markets.

DRIED: Does not air dry well, requires smoking. The dried Japonés are NOT dried Serranos.

PREPARED: Mexican pickled (*escabeche*) Serranos are occasionally found in specialty stores.

SEEDS: Catalogs of most large seed houses and specialty seed companies. Available cultivars: Altamira, Cuauhtemoc, Cotaxtla Cónico, Cotaxtla Gordo, Cotaxtla Típico, Hidalgo, Huasteco 74, Panuco, Serrano Chili, Tampiqueño.

USES Used green in table sauces, guacamole, relishes, vegetable dishes, as a seasoning or garnish; pickling.

REMARKS A very fresh, almost citrus flavor. This is the most used fresh pepper in Mexico, where it is used in the ubiquitous Salsa Cruda, a table sauce of tomatoes, onions, garlic, cilantro, and Serranos which is made fresh daily. Serranos were originally grown by highlanders (*serranos*) in Mexico. Because it does not dry well naturally, it is seldom found or used dried.

Capsicum frutescens

Tabasco, fresh

SIZE 1 to 1½ inches (2.5 to 3.8 cm) long; ¼ to ⅜ inches (.6 to 1 cm) wide.

COLOR Pale yellow-green to yellow to orange to red.

FRUIT SHAPE Elongate cylinder; pointed apex; obtuse at peduncle attachment; smooth cross section. Tabasco type.

FLESH Thin walled.

PUNGENCY Very high; 10.

SUBSTITUTES Chiltepín, Cascabella, Louisiana Sport, Mississippi Sport, Thai.

OTHER NAMES None.

SOURCES FRESH: Home garden.
DRIED: Not dried.
PREPARED: Pepper sauces made with Tabasco peppers abound; occasionally pickled whole peppers are available in food stores.
SEEDS: Specialty seed catalogs, a few major seed catalogs. The seed you get will probably be Greenleaf Tabasco. Available cultivars: Greenleaf Tabasco, Select, Tabasco.

USES In sauces, as a seasoning.

REMARKS The pepper from which Tabasco was selected came to Louisiana from the area which is now the state of Tabasco, Mexico, during the U.S. war with Mexico (1846–1847). The McIlhenny family had made a sauce they called tabasco sauce (now Tabasco Pepper Sauce®) from a pepper grown on Avery Island, Louisiana, before they fled during the Civil War. After the war they continued to make the sauce, and later the pepper was named Tabasco after the sauce. In the 1960's a wilt disease nearly wiped out the Tabasco. The Mississippi Sport and Louisiana Sport peppers substituted for Tabasco peppers until the disease-resistant Greenleaf Tabasco was developed. Neither Sport pepper is grown today. The McIlhenny Company has branched out beyond its world-famous original Tabasco Pepper Sauce.

Capsicum annuum var. *annuum*

Thai / Hang Prik, fresh and dried

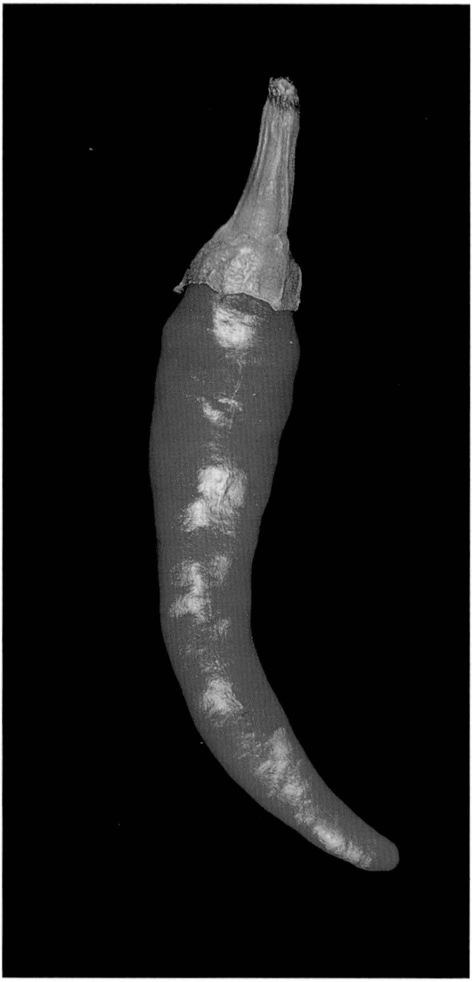

SIZE	3½ to 4 inches (8.9 to 10.2 cm) long; ½ to ¾ inch (1.3 to 1.9 cm) wide.
COLOR	Green to red.
FRUIT SHAPE	Elongate, tapering to a point, curved; obtuse at the peduncle attachment; cross section slightly corrugated. Cayenne type.
FLESH	Medium thick walled.
PUNGENCY	Intermediate to high; 6 to 10.
SUBSTITUTES	Cayenne, Jalapeño, Serrano.
OTHER NAMES	Thai pepper.
SOURCES	FRESH: Oriental food stores. DRIED: Oriental food stores. PREPARED: Oriental food stores. SEEDS: Specialty seed houses.
USES	In sauces, stir fry, curries, and most Thai or Indonesian dishes.
REMARKS	This looks like a Cayenne, but it is much more pungent. *Prik* is a Thai word for chilli (any pungent pepper). Thais add other words to their word for chilli to indicate whether it is fresh, dry, green, or red, such as *Prik Kenu, Prik Youk, Prik Laung.*

Capsicum annuum var. *annuum*

Tomato Pepper, fresh

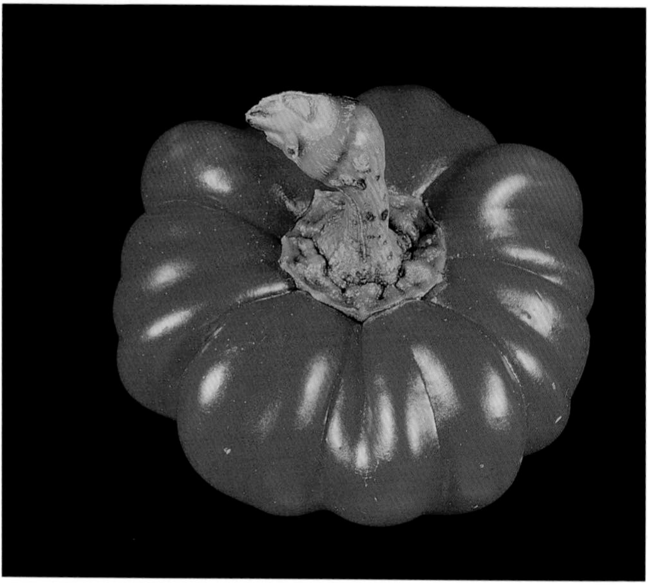

SIZE 3 inches (7.6 cm) in diameter.

COLOR Green to red.

FRUIT SHAPE Round, tomato-like, or white patty-pan squash shaped; sunken apex; lobate at peduncle attachment; very corrugated cross section. Tomato type.

FLESH Thick walled.

PUNGENCY Not pungent; 0 to 1.

SUBSTITUTES Pimento, red Bell pepper.

OTHER NAMES Paprika, Spanish Paprika, Squash pepper.

SOURCES FRESH: Home gardens, farmer's markets.
DRIED: Not used.
PREPARED: Canned, sold as pimento; pickled; commercial coloring agent; powdered.
SEEDS: Catalogs of most large seed companies. Available cultivars: Canada Cheese, Early Sweet Pimento, Sunnybrook, Tomato Pimento, Yellow Cheese Pimento.

USES Same as for Bell pepper; powdered, sold as paprika; canned as pimento; food and industrial coloring agent.

REMARKS When Europeans first discovered the New World tomato in the early sixteenth century, its many-lobed appearance was much like this pepper, hence the name. Look at still life paintings of the sixteenth and seventeenth century for examples of that early tomato. A very tasty sweet pepper.

Turkish, fresh and dried

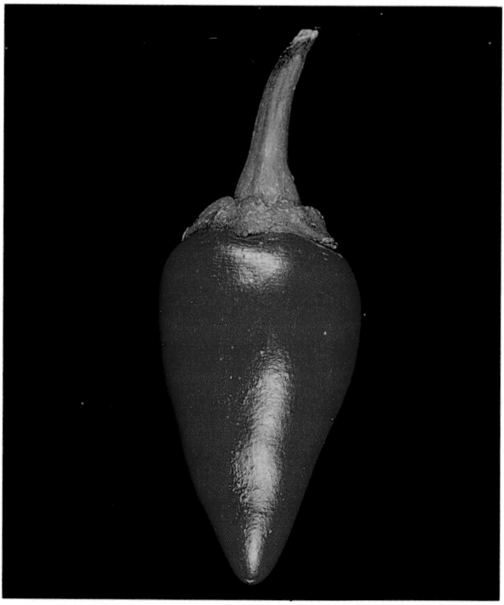

SIZE	2 to 3 inches (5.1 to 7.6 cm) long; ¾ to 1 inch (1.9 to 2.5 cm) wide at the shoulder.
COLOR	Green to red.
FRUIT SHAPE	Conical; truncate at peduncle attachment; smooth cross section. Small red wax type.
FLESH	Thin walled.
PUNGENCY	Intermediate to high; 5 to 7.
SUBSTITUTES	Pungent imported paprika; ground Anaheim/New Mexican Chile is less flavorful.
OTHER NAMES	Aleppo pepper; common name unknown; seed was collected in Turkey.
SOURCES	FRESH: Home gardens. DRIED: Ethnic food stores. PREPARED: Rare in ethnic food stores. SEEDS: Pick them out of packaged ground Turkish pepper or try Sunset Farms.
USES	Sprinkle on Middle Eastern, Mediterranean, Italian, or Latin American dishes—on anything. Seasoning for soups, stews, sauces, casseroles.
REMARKS	I found a delicious fairly mild ground pepper in the market at Urfa, Turkey. Having fallen in love with its flavor, I brought several kilos home with me. Most of the seed had been removed; however, I found enough that Richard and Robert Penn of Sunset Farms were able to grow them and dry them so we could have more ground pepper. On another trip I found the same or a similar ground pepper in Aleppo, Syria, which is not far from Urfa. A Middle Eastern food store in Boston sells this as "Aleppo pepper." Warning: can be severely habit forming—but good!

Capsicum chinense

West Indian Hot, fresh

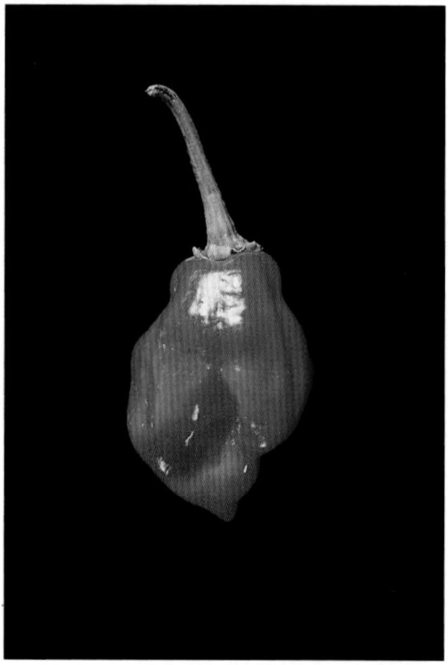

SIZE	1 to 2½ inches (2.5 to 6.4 cm) long; 1 inch (2.5 cm) wide.
COLOR	Green to red.
FRUIT SHAPE	Campanulate, undulating; pointed apex; truncated peduncle attachment; cross section has intermediate corrugation. Habanero type.
FLESH	Thin walled.
PUNGENCY	Very high; 10+.
SUBSTITUTES	Dátil, Habanero.
OTHER NAMES	No other name.
SOURCES	FRESH: Home gardens. DRIED: Not dried. PREPARED: Not processed yet. SEEDS: CARDI, Antigua, British West Indies.
USES	Table sauces or as you would use the Habanero.
REMARKS	I found this beautiful pepper growing in Antigua, British West Indies. Its breeder, Dr. Brian Cooper, the director of the Caribbean Agricultural Research Development Institute, gave me seed which I brought to central Texas, where Richard and Robert Penn of Sunset Farms found them easy to grow. The Red Savina Habanero looks very much like this pepper.

ILLUSTRATED GLOSSARY

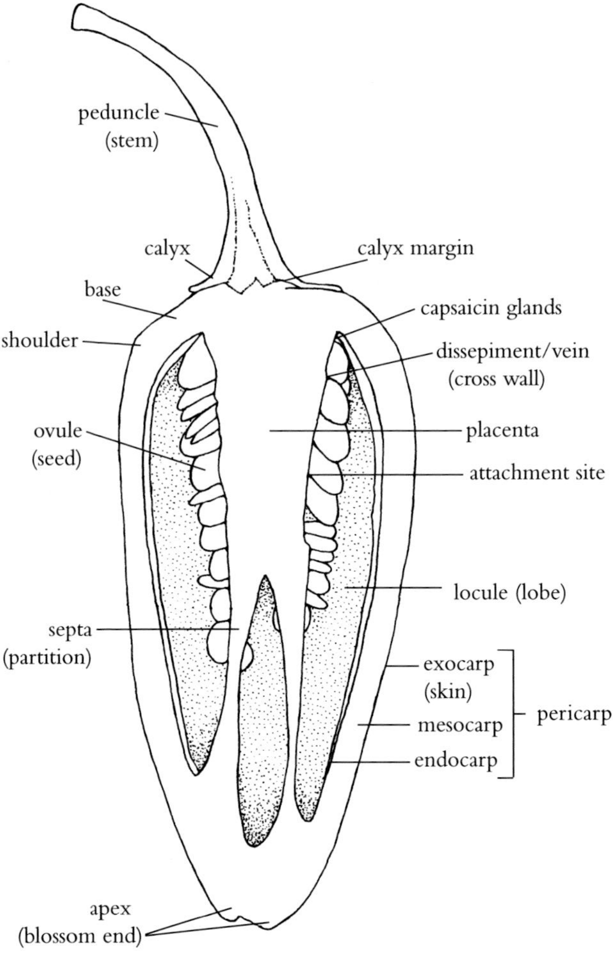

1. Cross section of a *Capsicum* fruit.

2. Fruit Outline

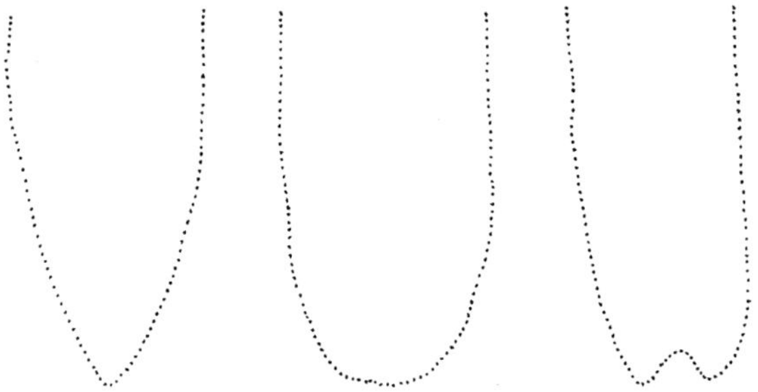

3. Fruit Shape at Apex

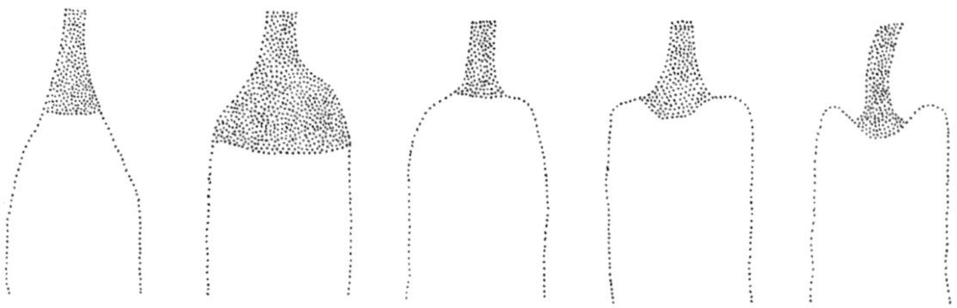

4. Fruit Shape at Peduncle Attachment

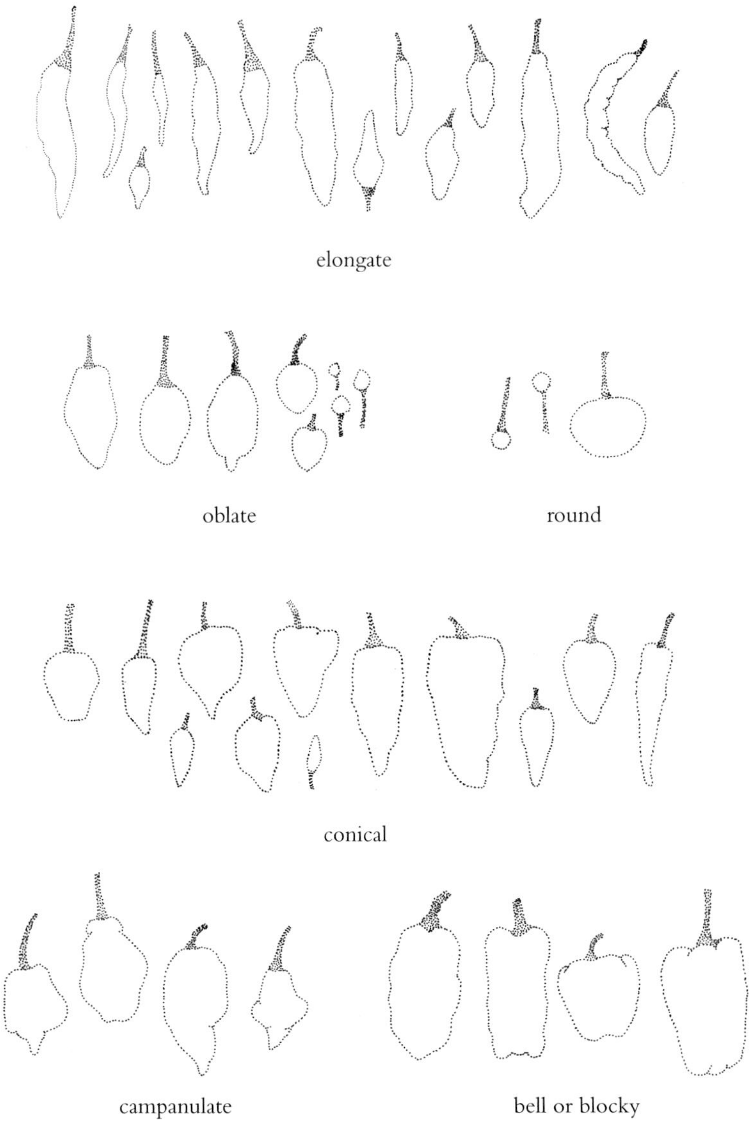

5. Fruit Shape

GLOSSARY

Achocolatado: Spanish, meaning reddish brown or chocolate colored.

Acuminate: Long and pointed, tapering.

Ají: Pronounced ah-hee. A name used in much of South America to denote pungent peppers. It was being used in the Caribbean island visited by Christopher Columbus on his voyages.

Anther: The part of the stamen in which pollen develops, borne at the tip of the filament.

Apex: Blossom end or tip of a fruit.

Base: The broadest portion of a cone-shaped pepper; the peduncle/stem is attached at the base of the fruit.

Berry: Pulpy, few- or many-seeded fruit; the pulpy fruit resulting from a single pistil, containing one or more seeds but no true stone; e.g., tomato, grape.

Blossom end: The part of the pepper where the blossom was attached; opposite the base; the apex.

Calyx: The outer circle of floral envelopes which attaches the peduncle to the fruit.

Campanulate: Bell-shaped.

CAPS: An abbreviation for capsaicin, the pungent principle in peppers.

Ceviche: An uncooked Latin American dish made from chopped seafood, principally fish, onions, cilantro, chilli peppers, lime juice, and variable other seasonings. The seafood is soaked for a long (4–12 hour) period in the lime juice, which "cooks" it before the other ingredients are added.

Chile: The Spanish form of the word *chilli* (capsicum peppers) used in Mexico; also a South American country.

Chili: The anglicized spelling of the word *chilli* used in the United States.

Chilli, chillies: The most used term, other than peppers, employed by English-speaking people worldwide. The Food and Agriculture Organization of the United Nations (FAO) uses *chilli* for the pungent capsicums and *peppers* for the nonpungent (sweet) ones.

Conical: Cone-shaped.

Cordate: Heart-shaped.

Corolla: Inner circle of floral envelopes; if the parts are separate, they are petals; if they are not separate, they are teeth, lobes, or divisions.

Corrugated: Furrowed, wrinkled; used to describe a cross section of the pepper fruit.

Cultivar: A variety or race that has originated and persisted under cultivation; not necessarily referable to botanical species.

Cultivated: To cultivate means to conduct human activities involving the care of a plant. Both wild and domesticated plants can be cultivated; genetic modification is not involved.

Deciduous: Falling, as the leaves, at the end of one season of life; as leaves of nonevergreen trees.

Dehiscence: The bursting or splitting open of a plant's seed pod, fruit, or anther at maturity.

Domestication: An evolutionary process operating under the influence of human activity. In plants there is genetic modification through selection. A domesticated type is usually incapable of survival without the care of humans.

Elongate(d): Extended, stretched; used to describe the shape of the fruit. Elongated cone, elongated cylinder.

Ethnic: Pertaining to races of people. An ethnic pepper is one favored by a certain group of people. Used primarily in reference to peppers favored by those of Balkan, Italian, and Turkish extraction.

Fruit: A structure incorporating one or more ripened ovaries, with or without seeds, and sometimes with accessory structures derived from other parts of the flower, as an apple, bean pod, nut, berry, melon, grain, pepper.

Globular: Shaped like a globe; spherical.

Güero: Blond, fair, golden; same as *rubio*. Yellow peppers are called *güeros*.

Lobate: Composed of or having lobes or sections resembling lobes.

Lobe: Any part or segment of an organ; specifically, a part of a petal or calyx or leaf that represents a division to about the middle.

Locule: A small lobe; compartment or cell of an ovary; a descriptive term lacking morphological meaning.

Mole: Fricassee of turkey or other meat with dark chilli sauce.

Nahuatl: The language spoken by certain Mexican Indian tribes at the time of the Conquest. It persists today among several million Mexicans.

Obtuse: Blunt, rounded.

Ovary: The part of the flower which develops into a fruit.

Ovate: With an outline like that of a hen's egg cut in two lengthwise.

Ovule: The body which after fertilization becomes the seed.

Pedicel: Stem of one flower in a cluster.

Peduncle: Stem of a flower cluster or of a solitary flower.

Peduncle attachment: The site on the base of the pepper where the peduncle or stem is attached.

Perennial: Continuing through the year; lasting more than three seasons.

Pericarp: The wall of a ripened ovary; wall of a fruit, sometimes used to designate fruit.

Petal: One of the separate leaves of a corolla.

Placenta: The structure by which an ovule (seed) is attached to the wall of the ovary.

Pod: The dry dehiscent fruit splitting along two sutures, as that of a legume (bean or pea). Pepper pods are berries, not true pods.

Pubescent: Covered with short, soft hairs; downy.

Pungent: A sensory response causing warm, mouth-watering effects, which result in greater acceptance and higher intake of the insipid basic nutrient foods. It should be the gustatory attribute of chillies, not hot, sharp, bite. It is a gustatory attribute of food, as are sweet, sour, bitter, saline. Chilli peppers are pungent, as are black pepper, mustard, ginger, and horseradish. The chemical compound producing pungency is different in each of the pungent foods: chilli—capsaicin, black pepper—piperine, ginger—ginerol, mustard and horseradish—sinigrin.

Registered cultivar: A cultivated variety of a plant which has been accepted by an international registration authority and the inclusion of this name in a register. When the cultivar name immediately follows a botanical or common name, it must be distinguished from the latter, either by placing the abbreviation cv. before the cultivar name, or by enclosing the name within single quotation marks. Ex.: *Capsicum chinense* cv. Red Savina; or *C. chinense* 'Red Savina.'

Scoville heat units: A term stemming from the Scoville Organoleptic Test of 1912, which was an oral method of determining the pungency of peppers. The results were expressed in Scoville Heat Units, which are still used by modern methods. Unfortunately these tests apply only to the specific pepper specimen tested.

Sessile: Not stalked.

Shoulder: The region of the pepper fruit below the calyx.

Translucent: Used in describing the dried pericarp of a pepper when one can see through it. Not all peppers are translucent when dried.

Truncate: Appearing to have a cut-off or squared apex.

Wax type: An extremely glossy or waxy pericarp or outer skin; usually yellow in one stage of maturity.

Wild: Has not been genetically manipulated by humans; however, it may be cultivated; may be spontaneous, not planted by humans.

SEED SOURCES

Enchanted Seeds
P.O. Box 6087, Las Cruces NM 88006

Horticultural Enterprises
P.O. Box 810082, Dallas TX 75381-0082

Native Seeds/SEARCH
2509 N. Campbell Ave. #325, Tucson AZ 85719
(catalog $1.00)
(A nonprofit conservation, education, and research organization; membership required.)

Petoseed Co., Inc. (wholesale)
P. O. Box 4206, Saticoy CA 93007-4206

The Pepper Gal (nothing but peppers)
P.O. Box 23006, Ft. Lauderdale FL 33307

Plants of the Southwest
930 Baca St., RR6, Box 11A, Santa Fe NM 87501-7806

Redwood City Seed Co. (wholesale & retail)
P.O. Box 361, Redwood City CA 94064

Shepherd's Garden Seeds
6116 Hwy 9, Felton CA 95018
also 30 Irene St., Tarrington CT 06790

Vermont Bean Seed Co.
Garden Lane, Bomoseen VT 05732

Seed Savers Exchange
3076 N. Winn Road, Decorah IA 52101

(*Useful*: Seed Savers Exchange is a membership organization whose members exchange seed. Send $1.00 for an information brochure. It publishes *The Non-Hybrid Garden Seed Inventory*, a computerized inventory of all non-hybrid garden seeds available by mail order in the USA and Canada, which lists more than 240 sweet peppers and more than 260 hot peppers.)

Don Alfonso (dried pepper importer)
P.O. Box 201988, Austin TX 78720-1988

(A large assortment from Mexico which can be used for cooking and for seed.)

Richard and Robert Penn
Sunset Farms/Gourmet Peppers
P.O. Box 4866, Lago Vista TX 78645

INDEX

Boldface page numbers indicate photographs.